T0334263

Celebrity Mad

This short book by Professor Brett Kahr provides a psychoanalytic understanding of fame and celebrity in the early twenty-first century, building upon the bedrock foundations of the Freudian corpus.

The book is divided into six chapters. Chapter One explores the psychology of the celebrity, questioning narcissistic and exhibitionist psychopathology, while Chapter Two examines the psychological state of those of who revel in the fame of others and in celebrity culture more broadly, and offers a discussion of the "Celebrity Worship Syndrome". Chapter Three provides a very brief history of the concept of celebrity itself, arguing that, contrary to popular opinion, the culture of celebrification cannot be blamed on twenty-first-century media moguls, but, rather, that such a preoccupation with famous personalities can be traced back to ancient times and demonstrates the need to broaden our analysis to include the role of deep, unconscious psychological forces. In Chapter Four, Kahr reviews some important theoretical concepts advanced by Freud and Winnicott, which provide an important foundation for the psychoanalytic study of fame, while Chapter Five provides a more comprehensive theory of the unconscious psychological roots of the need to worship fame and to seek it, drawing upon a multitude of sources, ranging from psychoanalytic theory and developmental psychological research, to film, archaeology, and, perhaps surprisingly, the history of infanticide. The book concludes, in Chapter Six, by studying the psychodynamics of celebrity and fame, arguing that being recognised by one's family and friends in the intimate context of home life may well be the very best way to become a celebrity.

Celebrity Mad outlines a psychoanalytic theory of the roots of our obsession with fame. It will be of great interest to psychoanalytic practitioners and researchers, as well as to readers interested in the psychology of fame.

Professor Brett Kahr has worked in the mental health field for over forty years. He is Senior Fellow at the Tavistock Institute of Medical Psychology in London and Senior Clinical Research Fellow in Psychotherapy and Mental Health at the Centre for Child Mental Health in London. A Trustee of the Freud Museum London and of Freud Museum Publications, he has written or edited fourteen books, and he has served as series editor for more than fifty-five other titles. He is Consultant Psychotherapist at The Balint Consultancy and works full-time with individuals and couples in London.

Books by Brett Kahr

D.W. Winnicott: A Biographical Portrait (1996)

Forensic Psychotherapy and Psychopathology:
  Winnicottian Perspectives, Editor (2001)

Exhibitionism (2001)

The Legacy of Winnicott:
  Essays on Infant and Child Mental Health, Editor (2002)

Sex and the Psyche (2007)

Who's Been Sleeping in Your Head?:
  The Secret World of Sexual Fantasies (2008)

Life Lessons from Freud (2013)

Tea with Winnicott (2016)

Coffee with Freud (2017)

New Horizons in Forensic Psychotherapy:
  Exploring the Work of Estela V. Welldon, Editor (2018)

How to Flourish as a Psychotherapist (2019)

Bombs in the Consulting Room:
  Surviving Psychological Shrapnel (2020)

On Practising Therapy at 1.45 A.M.:
  Adventures of a Clinician (2020)

Celebrity Mad

Why Otherwise Intelligent People Worship Fame

Brett Kahr

Routledge
Taylor & Francis Group

LONDON AND NEW YORK

First published 2020
by Routledge
2 Park Square, Milton Park, Abingdon, Oxon OX14 4RN

and by Routledge
52 Vanderbilt Avenue, New York, NY 10017

Routledge is an imprint of the Taylor & Francis Group, an informa business

British Library Cataloguing-in-Publication Data
A catalogue record for this book is available from the British Library

Library of Congress Cataloging-in-Publication Data
A catalog record has been requested for this book

ISBN: 978–1–78220–667–5 (pbk)
ISBN: 978–0–429–43893–6 (ebk)

Edited, designed, and typeset in Adobe Caslon Pro
by Communication Crafts, East Grinstead

To

Jane Ryan,
in recognition of her unparalleled capacity
to celebrate others

Praiſe, *is Devotion fit for mighty Mindes.*

Sir William D'Avenant, *Gondibert: An Heroick Poem,* 1651

CONTENTS

Introduction
"Oh, they have all outstripped me in fame":
Sigmund Freud's struggle with celebrity   1

Chapter One
"Envied and adored, and most wretchedly
unhappy": are all celebrities mad?   15

Chapter Two
"A mass masturbation orgy":
the celebrity worship syndrome   25

Chapter Three
"I woke up the next morning and found
myself famous": towards a history of notoriety   39

Chapter Four
"Mama getting out of the bathtub in the nude":
the roots of celebrification   51

Chapter Five
"Drag the sublime into the mud":
towards a more comprehensive theory of celebrity   61

Chapter Six
"I'm a celebrity and I don't even know it":
on becoming famous in one's own household   81

Notes   89

Acknowledgements   93

References   95

Index   117

Celebrity Mad

It is the veriest madness man
  In maddest mood can frame,
To feed the earth with human gore,
  And then to call it fame.

"Iole" [Letitia Elizabeth Landon], "Metrical Fragments—
No. 1", *The London Literary Gazette, and Journal of Belles
Lettres, Arts, Sciences, & c.*, 19 August, 1826

.

INTRODUCTION

"Oh, they have all outstripped me in fame": Sigmund Freud's struggle with celebrity

> Nichts ist greulicher als in das Tutehorn der allgemeinen
> bouillonwarmen Anerkennung zu stoßen.
> [Nothing is more detestable than to blow the horn of instant
> public acclaim.]
>
> Dr Carl Gustav Jung, Letter to Professor Sigmund Freud,
> 11 November 1908
> [Jung, 1908a, p. 195; Jung, 1908b, p. 176]

On 6 May 1939, the aged Professor Sigmund Freud, riddled with cancer, celebrated his eighty-third birthday at his home at 20, Maresfield Gardens, in Swiss Cottage, London, surrounded by his family. On that occasion, the weather proved sufficiently clement for the elderly psychoanalyst to have spent some of the time outdoors in the back garden of the house. But as the spring and summer unfolded, Freud's carcinoma enfeebled him increasingly, and so he retreated to his bedroom and began to prepare for death.

On 22 June 1939, Mrs Eva Grizzelle (1939), a 69-year-old woman from Le Roy, Illinois, sent Freud an unsolicited letter, explaining that a certain Dr Connell—probably

Walter Thomas Connell—had cured her of pancreatic cancer at a hospital in Canada with a specially devised serum. She strongly recommended that Freud should travel overseas to receive similar treatment. But Sigmund Freud certainly never did so. As Anna Freud—the youngest of his six children— often censored her father's correspondence protectively, we do not even know whether Freud read Mrs Grizzelle's letter.

By 1 August 1939, after more than sixty years of working with patients, Sigmund Freud ceased his clinical practice entirely, and on 6 August 1939, he bid farewell to his former analysand and long-standing friend and colleague, the Princesse Marie Bonaparte, who helped to rescue him from Nazi-infested Austria (Jones, 1957). Ordinarily, the devoted Princesse would have remained near-to-hand, but, at that time, she had to travel to Madras, in India, in order to attend the wedding of her only son, His Royal Highness Prince Petros, Prince of Greece and Denmark.

Eventually, Freud became too frail to remain in his first-floor bedroom, and so he moved into the ground-floor study, where he spent his final days reading, most aptly, Honoré de Balzac's novel *La Peau de chagrin: Roman philosophique*, in the original French, in an edition published in Vienna—a fantastical book about a man whose skin begins to shrink and shrivel (Balzac, n.d. [1920]).

Freud still maintained an interest in world events, and he certainly learned that, on 1 September 1939, Germany had invaded Poland, and that, two days later, on 3 September, both Great Britain—Freud's newly adopted country—and, also, France declared war on Germany. Having lived through the Austro–Prussian war of 1866 and then through the Great War of 1914–1918, the outbreak of yet another *Weltkrieg* would hardly have surprised the father of psychoanalysis, who had devoted much of his professional life to a careful study of the cruel underbelly of human nature.

As the month unfolded, political events became increasingly terrifying. On 5 September, King George VI gave royal assent to the National Registration Act 1939, which required each inhabitant of the United Kingdom to carry an identity card. And on 9 September, the Germans reached Warsaw. On the 17th of that month, a German submarine exploded the British cruiser *H.M.S. Courageous*, resulting in the deaths of 519 members of the crew. And on 20 September, Great Britain retaliated by sinking a German U-27.

Injected with morphine to dull his bodily pain, Freud eventually died at approximately three o'clock in the morning on Saturday, 23 September 1939, in the study of his London home (Schur, 1972), having suffered from cancer for more than a decade-and-a-half.

News of Freud's decease spread instantly across the world and received enormous coverage in the press and on the radio. Indeed, Freud's nephew, Harry Freud (n.d.), learned of his uncle's death while walking through Times Square in New York City. And the noted English psychiatrist Professor Denis Hill recalled that when the British Broadcasting Corporation announced Freud's passing on the wireless, a group of hardened working-class manual labourers in a pub in South London, near to the Maudsley Hospital, removed their ubiquitous cloth caps as a sign of respect (interview with Jonathan Pedder, 22 October 1996).

Sigmund Freud's life ended in 1939, amid a world very different from our own. He died never having watched television, or having searched the internet, or having drunk a cup of coffee from Starbucks. Indeed, Freud knew nothing of Facebook, YouTube, internet banking, cybersex, Twitter, e-mails, texting, Google, What's App, Instagram, or space travel.

He had never encountered microwaves, or credit cards, or air conditioning, or Botox, or Prozac, or the music of the Beatles or the Rolling Stones or Madonna, let alone heavy metal. He had never seen a memory stick or an iPhone or an iPad or an iPod, nor had he ever listened to music on iTunes. And he would have stared with amusement at a McDonald's hamburger and at Ben and Jerry's ice cream.

Indeed, it might have horrified him to know that his many carefully scripted books would be read one day, *not* in cloth-bound volumes but, rather, on a Kindle.

Furthermore, Freud did not have access to the wealth of medical data—now widely available—about the links between smoking and cancer. He had never visited a gym for a work-out; he had never used a laptop or, indeed, a standing-desk; and he certainly would have struggled to decipher initials such as C.C.T.V., C.D., D.V.D., I.V.F., and L.G.B.T.Q.

Although Freud had, of course, encountered Adolf Hitler, the founder of psychoanalysis had no idea of the unspeak-able insanity that would unfold throughout the early 1940s, nor could he have conceived that four of his elderly sisters would be exterminated in the Nazi death camps. And one can only imagine Freud's reaction to the news of the atom-bombing of Hiroshima and Nagasaki, not to mention the ghastliness of 9/11 and other incarnations of technologised terrorism.

If Sigmund Freud could be resurrected today and employed as a commentator on C.N.N.—the Central News Network—one wonders what he would understand about the current treatment of mental illness, about Brexit, about the global immigration crisis, about the conflict in Syria, or climate change, or even about Donald Trump?

And what would Freud have thought about our contemporary celebrity culture?

Most commentators on the nature of fame have provided rather inadequate engagements with the subject. As the British radio broadcaster Steve Allen (2015, p. 73) lamented, somewhat desperately, in his book *So You Want to Be a Celebrity?*: "Ah, if I could explain our fascination with celebrity, I'd earn a fortune", underscoring that one would really require the services of a psychologist in order to comprehend the nature of celebrity addiction more fully.

In this short essay, I shall endeavour to offer an understanding of our seemingly modern obsession with fame, wondering what Freud might have written had he lived into the twenty-first century. I hope, therefore, to provide in this little book a classical psychoanalytic conceptualisation of an important aspect of our modern world, and I trust that this text will draw upon the best of Freud's early ideas and demonstrate something of their relevance for our current era.

But let us begin our investigation with what Freud, himself, actually understood about fame and celebrity . . .

* * *

Although he lived a very modest life and rarely went out in the evenings, Sigmund Freud knew a great deal about the rich and the famous.

Over the course of a long career as a psychoanalyst, he treated or provided consultations to some of the wealthiest and most venerated individuals of the early twentieth century, including the composers Alban Berg (Grun, 1971; Oberlerchner and Tögel, 2015; cf. Berg, 1923) and Gustav Mahler (Freud, 1935), the ballet dancer Vaslav Nijinsky (Nijinsky, 1933), the opera singer Richard Tauber (Castle and

5

Tauber, 1971; Eissler, n.d.), the aristocrat Princesse Marie Bonaparte (Bertin, 1982), as well as the heiress Fanny Moser (Ellenberger, 1977; Tögel, 1999), and, also, the exceptionally rich art historian Aby Warburg (Chernow, 1993). Some of his patients, such as the American diplomat William Bullitt, would even arrive at Freud's office in a limousine (Roazen, 1993).

Freud learned a great deal about fame and celebrity not only from the lives of his well-known and well-heeled analysands, but also from the ways in which this topic penetrated the minds of his more ordinary patients. In his essay "Über die psychogenese eines Falles von weiblicher Homosexualität" ["The Psychogenesis of a Case of Homosexuality in a Woman"], Freud (1920b, p. 160) described his young lesbian patient's infatuation for an older woman as equivalent to "the first passionate adoration of a youth for a celebrated actress whom he regards as far above him, to whom he scarcely dares lift his bashful eyes".[1]

Sigmund Freud not only engaged with the question of fame in the consulting room, but he also studied many public figures from world history with intense dedication. Over the decades, he wrote monographs or essays on such noted personalities as Leonardo da Vinci (Freud, 1910a) and Johann Wolfgang von Goethe (Freud, 1917), and he offered more pithy comments about various contemporary political personalities as well. For example, in 1933, Freud published a statement about the German emperor, Kaiser Wilhelm II, who had suffered from birth with a crippled arm, although, in the interests of discretion, he did not mention the Kaiser by name. Freud (1933b, p. 66) wrote that,

> It is usual for mothers whom Fate has presented with a child who is sickly or otherwise at a disadvantage to try to compensate him for his unfair handicap by a superabundance of love.

In the instance before us, the proud mother behaved otherwise; she withdrew her love from the child on account of his infirmity. When he had grown up into a man of great power, he proved unambiguously by his actions that he had never forgiven his mother.[2]

In his private correspondence, Freud pontificated more freely about celebrated individuals. For instance, on 17 December 1936, Freud (1936) penned a letter to his disciple, Princesse Marie Bonaparte, about Edward VIII, the recently abdicated British monarch, theorising that he might be a latent homosexual who found his heterosexual "Potenz" [potency] from Mrs Wallis Simpson.

Yet Freud knew about fame not only from his patients and from his psychoanalytic investigations of celebrated personalities, but, also, more directly, from his own private wishes and professional struggles.

As a young physician, Freud already yearned for fame and began to experience intimations that, one day, he might well achieve such recognition. Indeed, on 17 November 1884, he wrote to his fiancée and future spouse Fräulein Martha Bernays about certain colleagues who had already begun to make a name for themselves in the world of medicine: "Oh, they have all outstripped me in fame, but not in happiness and not in contentment so long as you are going to be mine"[3] (Freud, 1884b, p. 127). But in spite of this arguably level-headed approach to fame, he lamented, years later, to his colleague Dr Wilhelm Fliess that he might not attain all that he had wished, and that, "The expectation of eternal fame was so beautiful"[4] (Freud, 1897b, p. 266).

Freud knew, of course, that he had become famous, at least as early as 1902, when he received his honorary professorship at the Universität zu Wien [University of Vienna]. As he explained to Fliess,

Public acclaim was immense. Congratulations and flowers already are pouring in, as though the role of sexuality has suddenly been officially recognized by His Majesty, the significance of the dream certified by the Council of Ministers, and the necessity of a psychoanalytic therapy of hysteria carried by a two-thirds majority in Parliament.[5] [Freud, 1902b, p. 457]

In the succeeding years, Freud's fame continued to grow. For instance, in 1909, while travelling on the North German Lloyd steamer *George Washington* from Bremen, Germany, to Hoboken, New Jersey, in the United States of America, he spied a cabin boy reading his book *Zur Psychopathologie des Alltagslebens: (Über Vergessen, Versprechen, Vergreifen, Aberglaube und Irrtum)* (Freud, 1904) [*The Psychopathology of Everyday Life: Forgetting, Slips of the Tongue, Bungled Actions, Superstitions and Errors*] (Jones, 1955).[6]

By 20 October 1928, Dr Ernest Jones (1928) wrote to tell Freud that the *Encyclopaedia Britannica* had asked him to write a biographical entry on the father of psychoanalysis. And by 1936, in his eightieth year, Freud's fame had become so immense that he received, quite literally, "knapsacks full of congratulatory messages" (Sterba, 1982, p. 154), which prompted him to enthuse, with a reference to the five Dionne children, born in Ontario in 1934, "Now I know how the Canadian quintuplets feel, only they were used to it from birth" (quoted in Sterba, 1982, p. 154).

By the time that Freud had escaped to England from the Nazis, he had become so famous that letters would reach him at his temporary home on Elsworthy Road in Primrose Hill, addressed quite simply, "Freud, London" (quoted in Martha Freud, 1938, p. 515).[7] Indeed, even Freud's new British bank manager enthused "I know all about you" (Sigmund Freud, 1938, p. 903).

Freud did not, however, enjoy his celebrity, which often turned into a more sinister form of notoriety. Indeed, as the progenitor of a new sexual psychology, he had attracted a considerable degree of hatred.

Because psychoanalysis had originated as a predominantly Jewish science, in a grossly anti-Semitic culture, Sigmund Freud long harboured deep anxieties about becoming too visible. The most brisk scrutiny of Ernest Jones's (1953, 1955, 1957) classic three-volume biography of Freud serves as a potent reminder that the father of psychoanalysis and his earliest Jewish followers had to endure an enormous amount of vilification when they presented their work in public and would often be dismissed as sexual deviants (cf. Kahr, 2009).

For instance, on 29 March 1910, Professor Wilhelm Weygandt, a much-venerated German psychiatrist, addressed a gathering of physicians in Hamburg and threatened to contact the vice-squad to arrest any sexually lubricious psychoanalysts (Embden, 1910). According to Dr Ernest Jones (1955, p. 116), Weygandt claimed that, "Freud's interpretations were on a level with the trashiest dream books. His methods were dangerous since they simply bred sexual ideas in his patients. His method of treatment was on a par with the massage of the genital organs."

Also at this time, Professor Joseph Collins, a former President of the American Neurological Association, publicly attacked his colleague Professor James Jackson Putnam, a Harvard University neurologist and an early American disciple of psychoanalysis, for having presented a paper which Collins caricatured as full of "pornographic stories about pure virgins" (quoted in Jones, 1910, p. 55). Indeed, Collins argued that the American Neurological Association must take a stand not only against "Freudism" (quoted in Jones, 1910, p. 55) but also Christian Science, supernaturalism, transcendentalism, and all other such "bosh, rot and nonsense" (quoted in Jones, 1910, p. 55). And when Dr Sándor Ferenczi, the pioneering Hungarian psychoanalyst, addressed a group of medical men in Budapest, a colleague who practised hydrotherapy—the treatment of neurotic illness through the use of therapeutic baths and douches—arose from his seat and began to vilify psychoanalysis as little more than "Schweinereien" (quoted in Ferenczi, 1911a, p. 354) ["hanky-panky" (quoted in Ferenczi, 1911b, p. 256)]. After the hydrotherapist had spoken, a dermatology colleague stood up, lambasted psychoanalysis as poisonous, and warned that, "Analysis is pornography; so analysts belong in jail"[8] (Ferenczi, 1911b, p. 256).

The many attacks on Freud and psychoanalysis left its founder feeling quite lonely and isolated. As he wrote to his colleague Dr Carl Gustav Jung, "Of course the negative aspect of my fame is even more pronounced; sometimes it annoys me that no one abuses you"[9] (Freud, 1910c, p. 378).

In view of the vitriol endured by the early psychoanalysts, one can hardly blame them for not having wished to engage more fully with the outer world; certainly, one can appreciate their reluctance to forge a dialogue with potentially crass popular culture. Freud, in particular, detested the media in all its many varieties, and he became very displeased when colleagues began to collaborate with the noted Austrian film-maker Georg Wilhelm Pabst in the making of an early dramatisation about psychoanalysis, the now famous silent movie *Geheimnisse einer Seele* [*Secrets of a Soul*], which débuted in Germany in 1926, following an erroneous 1925 report in *The New York Times* that Freud himself would direct the film! (Ries, 1995).

And not only did Freud refuse to collaborate with Georg Wilhelm Pabst, but, also, he turned down a lucrative offer from the Hollywood mogul Samuel Goldwyn to consult on a film about great lovers from history. Similarly, Freud declined to accept an extremely large sum of money from the American media magnate William Randolph Hearst to testify as an expert witness in the famous murder trial of Nathan Leopold, Jr and Richard Loeb (Jones, 1957; Kahr, 2005, 2007b).

Fame had even saved Freud's life. Had he not occupied such an internationally visible position, it seems most unlikely that the Nazis would have spared him. As it happened, Freud enjoyed special privileges unknown in the history of Jewry, having received permission to emigrate to London along with his wife, his children and their spouses, his housekeeper, and even his personal physician, Dr Max Schur, and his family. Moreover, Freud took his collection of antiquities and his furniture, as well as many of his books and papers. By contrast, the vast majority of Jews who did escape successfully from Nazi-occupied Austria fled with little more than the clothes on their backs.

Thus, Freud knew a great deal not only about the dangers but, also, the benefits of celebrity. And he understood something of the pleasures of fame and the burdens of infamy. Sigmund Freud maintained no illusions about his own notoriety, even confessing to his analysand Dr Roy Grinker (1940) that, after his death, he would become even more celebrated, owing to the fact that no one would then be able to attack him!

But what might Freud have understood about modern twenty-first-century celebrity culture had he lived past 1939? How might he have conceived the polemics of fame in an era when parading oneself in public seems, for many, a career path? What might he have written about such television programmes as *The Voice* and *The X Factor* and *American Idol*, which endeavour to manufacture overnight celebrities as mass entertainment? Would Freud have come to regard fame and celebrity as the ultimate expression of uninhibited individualism or, rather, as a symptom of the most grotesque form of pathological narcissism?

Although we cannot possibly conclude with any certainty how Freud would have approached the study of modern fame, this short essay attempts to provide a psychoanalytic understanding about fame and celebrity in the early twenty-first century, building upon the bedrock foundations of the Freudian corpus.

In the pages that follow, I shall outline a psychoanalytic theory of the roots of our obsession with fame. In Chapter One, I will explore the psychology of the celebrity, enquiring whether all famous people really do suffer from some form of narcissistic or exhibitionist psychopathology. Thereafter, in Chapter Two, I shall move beyond the realms of the mind of overtly famous people to a fuller examination of the psychological state of those of who revel in the fame of others and in celebrity culture more broadly, including those who succumb to a veritable "Celebrity Worship Syndrome".

In Chapter Three, I will offer a very brief history of the concept of celebrity itself, arguing that, contrary to popular opinion, the culture of celebrification cannot be blamed on twenty-first-century media moguls but, rather, that such a preoccupation with famous personalities can be traced back to ancient times. Such a simple observation underscores that the need for celebrities as objects to be used and abused may be quite deeply rooted in our very psychological fabric.

Although many theoreticians have argued that the lust for fame developed in the wake of the de-Christianisation of the Western world and, also, as a result of the rise of the media, I endeavour to demonstrate that we must broaden our analysis to include the role of deep, unconscious psychological forces. Thus, in Chapter Four, I shall review some important theoretical concepts advanced by Professor Sigmund Freud and Dr Donald Winnicott, which provide an important foundation for the psychoanalytic study of fame. In particular, we shall consider Freud's (1909a) notion of the family romance and Winnicott's (1969) concept of the use of the object, examining the ways in which celebrities become objects used by fans to satisfy primitive psychological wishes and needs.

In Chapter Five, I will attempt to provide a more comprehensive theory of the unconscious psychological roots of the need to worship fame and to seek fame, drawing upon a multitude of sources, ranging from psychoanalytic theory and developmental psychological research, to film, archaeology, and, perhaps surprisingly, the history of infanticide. I will endeavour to trace the ways in which our obsession with fame allows us to defend and protect ourselves against loss and impotence and how it permits us to master our own very profound anxieties about death.

In Chapter Six, I shall conclude this brief study of the psychodynamics of celebrity and fame by arguing that being recognised by one's family and friends in the intimate context of home life may well be the very best way to become a celebrity.

ONE

"Envied and adored, and most wretchedly unhappy": are all celebrities mad?

Who grasped at earthly fame,
Grasped wind: nay worse, a serpent grasped that through
His hand slid smoothly, and was gone; but left
A sting behind which wrought him endless pain.

Robert Pollok, *The Course of Time: A Poem, in Ten Books*,
1827, Book III, lines 533–536

Some years ago, I attended a very lavish, intimate dinner party in London's Notting Hill. The guest list consisted of a noted theatrical director, a nationally renowned broadcaster, a best-selling novelist, a multi-multimillionaire financier, an astronaut who had commanded one of the Apollo rocket ships, and an internationally venerated classical musician, whom, for reasons of confidentiality, I shall call "Maestro X". The assembled personalities proved so glittering that I recognised all the names beforehand, bar my own!

In spite of the elegant décor and the extremely delicious food, meticulously prepared by our gracious and solicitous hostess, I had a dreadful evening.

Whenever any particular subject arose in conversation, Maestro X dominated the discussion. In the midst of debating the Middle East, we soon learned that this venerable conductor had performed there many times, and that he knew more about Israeli politics than Benjamin Netanyahu. When we progressed to a discussion of cinema, Maestro X regaled us with his recent work in Hollywood and told us precisely what inner forces had prompted Steven Spielberg to film *Schindler's List*. And when we turned our attention to psychoanalysis, the Maestro certainly knew more about Sigmund Freud than I did, and he proceeded to pontificate in emphatic tones about why Freud had become a dinosaur.

I sat next to the astronaut, and, never having previously met anyone who had walked on the surface of the moon, I dared to switch the topic of conversation in a vain effort to include this rather timid and understated space voyager, who looked increasingly bored. Before the astronaut could clear his throat, Maestro X launched into a disquisition about the future of space travel and about his hopes of conducting an interplanetary concert one day. Indeed, Maestro X, an undeniably accomplished gentleman, supreme in his craft, and by far the most celebrated figure at the dining room table, held court all evening, but he did so in the most grandiose and narcissistic manner and turned what might otherwise have proved to be an extremely enjoyable supper party into a cross between a press conference and a Shakespearean monologue.

More recently, my wife and I had supper with a long-standing, cherished friend, who happens to be a prominent show business agent. Although he usually keeps his telephone switched off during our dinners, on this occasion he forewarned us that our meal might be interrupted by a highly demanding new client whose name he mentioned, and whom we recognised instantly as one of the most famous recording artists in world history.

Regrettably, I had another terrible evening.

The client in question, "Miss Y", stood to earn £40,000 for a very brief personal appearance, which required no singing and no preparation, and which would bring her enormous positive press coverage; yet Miss Y found the terms and conditions not entirely convivial, and so she continued to telephone the agent at five-minute intervals, screaming and hollering. The cell phone rang literally twenty times during our meal, and with each successive call our friend the agent came closer and closer to experiencing a cerebral haemorrhage. Eventually, the agent turned off his mobile telephone. Shortly thereafter, he fired the client, even though he had stood to earn a great deal of money in commission fees.

During these fraught suppers, Maestro X and Miss Y displayed far more narcissistic psychopathology than patients with whom I have worked, whom colleagues had referred *specifically* for narcissistic personality disorder. Indeed, the Maestro and the pop singer reminded me very much of the famous anecdote concerning the screen star Marlene Dietrich. Apparently, when some friends came backstage to see Miss Dietrich after a live concert performance, she reputedly boasted about how much she had enjoyed her own singing during the first act, how much she had delighted herself in the *second* act, and how beautiful she looked in her sparkling dresses. Then she turned to her friends and intoned, "But enough about me . . . what did *you* think of my performance?"

The narcissism of celebrities has certainly annoyed many people over the years. For instance, back in 1924, the author Virginia Woolf (1924, p. 120) lamented, in a letter, about one of her colleagues: "I met that surly devil Bunny Garnett; and really, his fame has congested him. He is rigid with self importance."

Noël Coward, actor, stage star, screen star, playwright, novelist, songwriter, singer, director, and painter, knew more about celebrities and their inner lives than perhaps any other diarist of the twentieth century. In 1955, Coward's great friend, the aforementioned Marlene Dietrich, performed her cabaret before an expensive audience at the Café de Paris in London. Afterwards, Miss Dietrich entertained Mr Coward in her suite at the Dorchester Hotel. Coward (1955a, p. 277) found Dietrich "fairly tiresome", and he wrote in his diary,

> She was grumbling about some bad Press notices and being lonely; she also gave an account of singing privately for the Queen, which was obviously meant to be highly amusing but merely turned out to be silly and bad-mannered. Poor darling Marlene. Poor darling glamorous stars everywhere, their lives are so lonely and wretched and frustrated. Nothing but applause, flowers, Rolls-Royces, expensive hotel suites, constant adulation. It's too pathetic and wrings the heart. [Coward, 1955a, p. 277]

Exactly one week later, Coward went to watch his even greater friends, Sir Laurence Olivier and his wife Vivien Leigh, Lady Olivier, star in William Shakespeare's *Macbeth* in Stratford-upon-Avon. After the stellar couple shone as "Macbeth" and "Lady Macbeth", they invited Coward back to their home, Notley Abbey, in Haddenham, Buckinghamshire, for the evening, where Coward (1955b, p. 278) "observed, to my true horror, that Vivien is on the verge of another breakdown." According to Coward (1955b, p. 278),

> She talked at supper wildly. She is obsessed, poor darling, by the persecutions of the Press; her voice became high and shrill and her eyes strange. This morning when she had gone to a fitting, Larry came and talked to me. He is distraught and deeply unhappy. Apparently this relapse has been on the way for some time. She has begun to lose sleep again and make scenes and invites more and more people to Notley until there is no longer any possibility of peace. Their life together is really hideous and

here they are trapped by public acclaim, scrabbling about in the cold ashes of a physical passion that burnt itself out years ago. I am desperately sorry because I love them both and I am truly fearful of what may happen. The cruelty of fifth-rate journalists has contributed a lot to the situation but the core of the trouble lies deeper, where, in fact, it always lies, in sex. She, exacerbated by incipient TB, needs more and more sexual satisfaction. They are eminent, successful, envied and adored, and most wretchedly unhappy.

Having had similar encounters with other stars throughout the course of his career, Coward (1958, p. 384) despaired, "It is sad to think how many of our glamorous leading ladies are round the bend."

Years later, after Miss Leigh's death, Laurence Olivier, now Baron Olivier of Brighton, revealed his own proto-narcissistic state of mind while speaking with the American actor Frank Langella on the set of the 1979 film *Dracula*. During an off-camera moment, Lord Olivier admired the physique of his younger co-star and confessed, "I had a lovely chest when I was your age. In fact, one of my fantasies was to be standing on a pedestal in a museum and have people pay to worship my naked form" (quoted in Langella, 2012, p. 72). Unsurprisingly, the equally self-absorbed Mr Langella (2012, p. 72) replied, "You too?"

The British-born actor Robert Pattinson, best known for his appearances in films such as *Harry Potter and the Goblet of Fire* and, also, *Twilight*, pontificated, "Pretty much every person I know who's got famous is completely nuts. It's just isolation and also the repetitiveness of your interactions with people" (quoted in Day, 2017, p. 19). Pattinson's musings, published in *The Telegraph Magazine*, certainly echo the more private remarks offered by Noël Coward many decades previously.

Not only do celebrities regard themselves as mad, but numerous psychological professionals also maintain a similar view about those people in the public eye. Indeed, shortly after I had begun to work in the media as a sometime broadcaster and television presenter on mental health issues, a very eminent psychologist forewarned me that I would soon come to discover that every single famous individual suffers from borderline personality disorder. He told me that I would not believe this fact at first, yet after a period of years, I have come to appreciate that this hard-won clinical observation contains a great deal of truth.

Having now worked in the media for nearly forty years, I have had the privilege of meeting and, often, collaborating with, those who have achieved international fame, as well as those who have had more modest walk-on parts in crowd scenes; and although I have, in fact, encountered several people who have met the diagnostic criteria for borderline personality disorder or narcissistic personality disorder, I have come to know many more who do not. Indeed, I have discovered that working with "famous" people and with "celebrities" in a clinical context proves to be a most fulfilling experience, because famous people often become the best psychotherapy patients, and they usually work extremely well in treatment. Having already survived the pains and the pleasures of being scrutinised by the entire world, they experience the benign camera lens of the psychotherapist or psychoanalyst as a great relief. They also live in a world in which everyone has struggled with drugs, alcohol, sexuality, violence, anxiety, and depression, and in which everyone admits to these conflicts quite *openly*; therefore, in my experience, many celebrities struggle much *less* with shame than ordinary neurotic patients do.

I could, of course, speak at greater length about the psychology of the celebrity, addressing questions concerning grandiosity, exhibitionism, and related topics, but I shall not do so, for two reasons. First of all, the pledge of confidentiality that each mental health practitioner promises implicitly or explicitly to each client must be sacrosanct and should remain so, even after the death of the psychotherapist. Second of all, although we might experience a sense of titillation when hearing about Madonna's preoedipal conflicts, Sting's psychosexual development, or Lady Gaga's struggles with the rapprochement subphase of the separation-individuation process, I suspect that we might be able to pose a much more interesting and much more important set of psychological questions, as part of a broader cultural analysis.

In 1996, Nathan Lane, the charismatic American theatre star, received a Tony Award for Best Actor in a Musical for his performance as "Pseudolus" in the Broadway revival of *A Funny Thing Happened on the Way to the Forum*. During his acceptance speech at the Majestic Theatre in Manhattan, Lane exclaimed, "this means a lot to me because as you know I'm an emotionally unstable, desperately needy little man." The packed audience of theatre professionals erupted in chortles, knowing that Lane's description of himself could readily apply to many others in the auditorium as well.

Of course, not every celebrity has become consumed by his or her international notoriety. In 1931, Harold Nicolson, the future British parliamentarian, recorded a charming anecdote in his diary about a luncheon party attended by such members of the aristocracy as Sir Oswald Mosley—the future leader of the British Union of Fascists—and others, such as Elizabeth, the Viscountess Castlerosse, and Lady Diana Cooper, the daughter of Henry Manners, the eighth

Duke of Rutland, not to mention the writer Herbert George Wells and the film star Charlie Chaplin. As Nicolson (1931, p. 93) recalled:

> We discuss fame. We all agree that we should like to be famous but that we should not like to be recognised. Charlie Chaplin told us how he never realised at first that he was a famous man. He worked on quietly at Los Angeles staying at the athletic club. Then suddenly he went on holiday to New York. He then saw "Charlie Chaplins" everywhere—in chocolate, in soap, on hoardings, "and elderly bankers imitated me to amuse their children". Yet he himself did not know a soul in New York. He walked through streets where he was famous and yet unknown.

Clearly, one can be famous without always realising that this might be the case. Such an anecdote certainly encapsulates an ostensibly less exhibitionistic and narcissistic relationship to fame in a film star.

One could readily investigate the deep unconscious characterological aspects and motivational strands that contribute to the development of the celebrity and, likewise, one could also examine the impact of fame and fortune upon the celebrity. Although we might imagine their lives to be a never-ending stream of banquets and balls, many celebrities also suffer profoundly from envious attacks and from bitter rivalries. Let us consider, for example, the noted playwright, screenwriter, and theatrical director Arthur Laurents, best known, perhaps, for having written the book for the perennial musical *West Side Story*. In his posthumously published memoir, Laurents recalled that fame had brought him a barrage of vicious anonymous messages, left on his answering machine, such as "*Do you know how many people hate you?*" (quoted in Laurents, 2012, p. 85) and "*Haven't you died yet?*" (quoted in Laurents, 2012, p. 85).

Everyone appreciates that celebrities struggle with psychological issues and illnesses and, also, with the ugly shadow side of being famous. But what about the *audience* members who pay to watch the celebrities display their inner worlds?

In the pages that follow, I will address no further the question of whether celebrities might be psychopathologically disturbed, attention-seeking, maternally deprived exhibitionists, or whether they suffer from the stresses of the institution of celebrity itself. In fact, I shall focus *not* on the celebrities but, rather, upon the audience—*you and me*—to begin to understand why we, as onlookers, become so obsessed with the lives of our celebrities. What role or roles do celebrities serve within our inner worlds? What function or functions do celebrities fulfil in terms of the unconscious life of the large group that we inhabit?

The Nielsen Company reported that, in 2013, the average American person watched approximately 155 hours and 32 minutes of television per month (including television programmes transmitted not only on T.V. sets but, also, on computers and cell phones) (*Advertising and Audiences: State of the Media. May 2014*, 2014). This constitutes almost the exact amount of time that one might devote to full-time employment! And much, if not most, of what we watch on television contains appearances and performances by celebrities, or news items about celebrities.

To quote but one memorable example: on 19 February 2010 the American golf champion Tiger Woods participated in a press conference in which he decided to apologise to the entire world for having cheated on his wife. One wonders why Mr Woods felt that he must deal with an essentially private marital matter on a global stage. But whatever Woods's motivations, or those of his managers and publicists, why do millions and millions, if not billions, of us watch these tele-confessions with such assiduity? So many people sat glued to their televisions that, according to C.N.N., trading on the New York Stock Exchange actually dipped during Tiger Woods's speech and then picked up again as soon as the press conference ended.

Let us now attempt to understand why we have become so obsessed with celebrity culture.

TWO

"A mass masturbation orgy": the celebrity worship syndrome

Fame is the ſpur that the clear ſpirit doth raiſe
(That laſt infirmity of noble mind)
To ſcorn delights, and live laborious days;
But the fair guerdon when we hope to find,
And think to burſt out into ſudden blaze,
Comes the blind Fury with the abhorred ſhears,
And ſlits the thin-ſpun life.

John Milton, "Lycidas", 1637,
lines 70–76

One need be neither a mental health professional nor a cultural commentator to appreciate our deep preoccupation with fame, with the famous, with those who had once enjoyed fame, with those who wish to become famous, with those earmarked for fame, and with those who had once had fame, then plummeted into obscurity, and then became famous once again—such as Gloria Stuart, a huge American film star of the 1930s, who retired, then virtually disappeared from view before resurfacing once more, decades later, in James Cameron's 1997 blockbuster film *Titanic*, for which she received an Academy Award nomination at the age of 87 years. We have become obsessed with those who have achieved fame for their great deeds, as well as those who have become famous for their notorious crimes, and, moreover, with those who have acquired fame simply for being famous. We relish details of the lives of those who garner fame overnight, such as the British television song-bird Susan Boyle, as well as those who had toiled for a lifetime, such as Mother Teresa. We cannot escape the famous. They fill our stages and our screens, our radios, newspapers, magazines, advertisements, and, most especially, our televisions, which I have come to think of as the veritable "cathode nipple" (Kahr, 2014, p. 31) upon which we suckle in order to obtain very primitive comfort.

And we pay our celebrities vast quantities of money so that they may continue to be celebrities. A reliable source who has worked behind the scenes on the television programme *American Idol* has told me in a personal communication that Simon Cowell, the internationally renowned celebrity judge, earns $27,000,000 per episode of this hit show, with sponsorship deals from major international corporations such as the Coca-Cola Company, the Ford Motor Company, Kellogg, and Clairol. Some years ago, *The Sunday Times Rich List 2010* (Beresford, 2010) claimed that Cowell boasted a fortune of £165,000,000, placing him in joint-398th place, as one of the richest individuals in Great Britain; and a more recent report has estimated Cowell's net worth at some $550,000,000 (Shelton, 2016), which seems to be rising all the time. Thus, the figure reported by my informant may well be accurate.

We all seem to crave a piece of celebrity, quite literally. According to a report about the auctioning of celebrity memorabilia, published in the *Financial Times*, back in 1999, someone paid £27,600—roughly the equivalent of the annual salary of a contemporary Briton—for a bull whip carried by Harrison Ford in one of the "Indiana Jones" action and adventure films. Another punter lavished $398,500 at a 1994 Christie's auction in New York City for the actual statuette used in the classic 1941 *film noir, The Maltese Falcon,* starring Humphrey Bogart. In all likelihood, the props department at Warner Brothers had manufactured the falcon in question out of *papier-mâché,* costing perhaps less than $1. Still another celebrity collector paid $660,000 to Christie's in 2000 for the ruby-red slippers worn by Judy Garland as "Dorothy Gale" in the 1939 film *The Wizard of Oz* (Griffin, 2003). And in 2016, someone spent over $4,810,000 for the shimmering white dress worn by Marilyn Monroe while she sang "Happy Birthday" to the American President John Fitzgerald Kennedy at Madison Square Garden in Manhattan, back in 1962 (Marilyn Monroe: 17, 18 & 19 November 2016, Los Angeles, C.A. Auction Results, 2016).

We cannot turn on our television sets or open up a copy of the *Radio Times* without being bombarded by an avalanche of programmes that exalt celebrities or promise that ordinary men and women might become celebrities too. In the absence of boasting a special talent, many a person will aspire to become a mere "micro-celebrity" (Marwick, 2013, p. 10), through an on-line presence as a blogger or through participation in one of the spate of so-called "reality television" programmes.

In recent years, the entertainment industry has bombarded viewers with this genre, having discovered that one can earn a great deal more money by filming ordinary members of the public than by paying large fees to professional actors. Such programmes have included: *The X Factor; I'm a Celebrity . . . Get Me Out of Here!; I'm a Celebrity: Jungle Royalty; I'm a Celebrity . . . Jungle Gold; Popstars; Dancing with the Stars; Pop Idol; American Idol; American Idol: Idol*

Gives Back; *America's Got Talent*; *Britain's Got Talent*; *Britain's Got More Talent*; *Stars in Their Eyes*; *Star Search*; *School for Stars*; and *The Voice UK*.

And let us not forget *Celebrity Fit Club*; *Celebrity Fat Camp*; *Celebrity Detox*; *The Celebrity Bank Job*; *Celebrity Deal or No Deal*; *Celebrity Juice*; *Celebrity Juice: Christmas Special*; *Celebrity Juice: X Factor Special*; *Celebrity Juice: Coronation Street Special*; *Celebrity Juice: 2041—A Juice Odyssey*; *Celebrity Juicemas Carol: Part 1*; *Celebrity Juice: Corrie vs. EastEnders*; *Celebrity Duets*; *Celebrity Four Weddings*; *Celebrity Wedding Planner*; *Celebrity Wife Swap*; *The Celebrity Apprentice*; *The Celebrity Apprentice USA*; *Celebrity Wish List*; *Celebrity Antiques Road Show*; *Celebrity Antiques Road Trip*; *Celebrity Big Brother*; *Celebrity Big Brother: Live Launch*; *Celebrity Big Brother: Live from the House*; *Celebrity Big Brother: Live Eviction*; *Celebrity Big Brother: Live Nominations*; *Celebrity Big Brother: The Final*; *Celebrity Big Brother: Live Final*; *Celebrity Big Brother: The Winner's Story*; *Celebrity Big Brother's Bit on the Side*; *Celebrity Big Brother: The Inside Story*; *Celebrity Big Brother: The Big Twist—Live*; and *National Celebrity Games*.

And no list would be complete without *Drop the Celebrity*; *Stars Behind Bars*; *Celebrity Alcatraz*; *10 Cutest Celebrity Babies: The Shortlist*; *40 Naughtiest Celebrity Scandals*; *40 Greatest Celebrity Slimdowns*; *World's Greatest Celebrity Body Shockers*; *Celebrity Go Home*; *Celebrity Place in the Sun*; *Celebrity B**** Slap News*; *Celebrity MasterChef*; *Celebrity MasterChef Australia*; *Celebrity MasterChef Goes Large*; *Celebrity Come Dine with Me*; *Celebrity Come Dine with Me Extra Portions*; *Come Dine with Me: Celebrity Special*; *Come Dine with Me: Celebrity Christmas Special*; *Celebrity Come Dine with Me: Ireland*; *Celebrity Pressure Cooker*; *Celebrity Mastermind*; *Celebrity Eggheads*; *Celebrity Bedlam*; *Celebrity Bites*; *Celebrity Britain's Best Dish*; *Celebrity Fantasy Homes*; *Celebrity First Dates*; Celeb-

rity Grimefighters; Celebrity DIY with Craig Phillips; Celebrity Ghost Stories UK; Celebrity Crises: 10 Most Shocking Mental Disorders; Celebrity Medical Nightmares: In Their Own Words; 40 Most Shocking Celebrity Divorces; 40 Most Slimmed-Down Celebs; Most Shocking Celebrity Moments 2010; Celebrity Are You Smarter Than a 10 Year Old; Top 50 Celebrity Meltdowns; Cash in the Celebrity Attic; 101 Biggest Celebrity Oops; 101 Even Bigger Celebrity Oops; Celebs on Benefits: Fame to Claim; Bankrupt and Broke: When Celebs Go Bust; Live Celebrity Who Wants to Be a Millionaire?; Celebrity Who Wants to Be a Millionaire?: New Year Special; Live Celebrity Who Wants to Be a Millionaire?: Mother's Day Special; and Celebrity Who Wants to Be a Millionaire?: Pantomime Special.

And in the interest of comprehensiveness, let us also pause to remember *America's Next Top Model; Fame Academy; Comic Relief Does Fame Academy; Fame and Fortune; How to Be Famous; When Will I Be Famous?; Famous and Fearless; Fame in the Frame; Wall of Fame; You've Been Framed and Famous!; The Model Agency; How to Kill a Celebrity; Celebrity, 24/7; Celebrity Coach Trip; Celebrity Exposed; Celebrity Naked Ambition; Celebrity Rehab; Celebrity Rehab with Dr Drew; Celebrity Super-Spa; Celebrity Fifteen to One; Pointless Celebrities; Pointless Celebrities: Comic Relief Special; Pointless Celebrities: Children in Need Special; Celebrity Five Go to . . .; Celebrity Slimdowns: Losing the Weight; Celebrity Charts; Celebrity Body Parts; All New Celebrity Total Wipeout; The Real Hustle: Celebrity Scammers; The Chase: Celebrity Special; The Cube: Celebrity Special; Most Shocking Celebrity Moments of 2011; All Star Family Fortunes; Star Academy; Star Academy Arab World; Remote Control Star; The Talent Show Story; Got to Dance: Auditions; Got to Dance: Auditions Uncut; All Star Mr and Mrs*; as well as *Celebs, Brands and Fake Fans*, and let us not forget *Alan Carr's Celebrity Ding Dong*, and *Famous, Rich and in the Slums*, as well as *Jack Osbourne: Celebrity Apprentice Junkie*, Series One, and, also, *Jack Osbourne: Celebrity Apprentice Junkie*, Series Two. Jaded and overfed on a constant diet of celebrity-orientated tripe, the British comedian Peter Kay wittily spoofed this trend in television commissioning with his own programme, entitled *Peter Kay's Britain's Got the Pop Factor . . . and Possibly a New Celebrity Jesus Christ Soapstar Superstar Strictly on Ice.*

Even members of the cultural aristocracy have succumbed to the temptation to contribute to the proliferation of overnight celebrity. The theatrical composer and impresario Andrew Lloyd Webber, Baron Lloyd Webber of Sydmonton, courted enormous controversy in the press and among the members of the entertainment industry by subverting the conventional casting process of numerous West End musical revivals, recruiting newcomers from the ranks of the general public and turning them into overnight stars, courtesy of the British Broadcasting Corporation, at taxpayer expense, with his television programmes *How Do You Solve a Problem Like Maria?*; *Any Dream Will Do*; *I'd Do Anything*; *Over the Rainbow*; and *Superstar*.

One television programme, in particular, has perhaps best captured the imagination of the public and its wish both to promote and to venerate celebrities and, also, to humiliate them—namely, *I'm a Celebrity . . . Get Me Out of Here!* This remarkably popular series provides a slightly different twist to the many other fame-orientated television events. Unlike the *American Idol* programme and the *Fame Academy* programme, for example, which propose to make stars out of unknown people, *I'm a Celebrity . . . Get Me Out of Here!* recruits already established personalities (whether so-called A-listers, B-listers, C-listers, or D-listers) and transforms them into even better-known personalities, who often leave the show with large advertising contracts. This television series has now graced our screens for nineteen seasons (and counting), garnering as many as 14.99 million viewers, or roughly one-third of the adult population of the United Kingdom. (Interestingly, as a point of comparison, the historic televised debate among Prime Ministerial candidates Gordon Brown, David Cameron, and Nick Clegg, broadcast on 15 April 2010, attracted a mere 10.4 million people). The celebrities who elect to go to the Australian Bush, where they must perform all sorts of complex tasks, including eating worms of various descriptions, have included Carol Thatcher, daughter of former Prime Minister Margaret Thatcher; Lauren Booth, sister-in-law of former Prime Minister Tony Blair; sporting stars Martina Navratilova and Phil Tufnell; pop star Jason Donovan; and broadcasters Jennie Bond (former Royal Correspondent for the British Broadcasting Corporation) and Esther Rantzen. The series has even spawned international spin-offs, such as France's *Je suis une célébrité—sortez-moi de là!*, and Germany's *Ich bin ein Star—Holt mich hier raus!*

Even if we try to escape the world of celebrity, we fail utterly. On a recent weekend mini-break to Paris, my wife and I checked into a little hotel off the Champs-Élysées, and upon entering our charming room, we found that the management had already turned on the television before our arrival, as though we might not be able to manage without it. To my surprise, I found myself confronted immediately with a television programme called *La Ferme: Célébrités en Afrique* [*The Farm: Celebrities in Africa*], undoubtedly a spin-off of the aforementioned British programme. After turning off the television in our room, we went for a stroll along a boulevard and within minutes found ourselves in front of a shop selling neither *baguettes* nor *fromages* but, rather, baby clothes, trading under the name *Une Étoile est née* [*A Star is Born*]. It would appear that even French babies must now begin life as celebrities-in-training.

Politicians, too, in spite of their profound, all-enveloping responsibilities, still find time to venerate or to hobnob with celebrities. For instance, Sir Alec Douglas-Home, the British Prime Minister, praised the Beatles as "our best exports" (quoted in Davies, 1968, p. 212). And when John Lennon, one of the Beatles, visited Canada in 1969, Pierre Trudeau, the Prime Minister, granted the British singer a fifty-minute audience (Norman, 2008).

In fact, in many instances, an association with show business has now become almost a prerequisite for a career in politics—witness the successful campaign of actress Glenda Jackson for a seat in the British Parliament, following a venerable American tradition that began when song-and-dance man George Murphy, an Academy Award-winning star of Hollywood musicals who had performed alongside Fred Astaire, Judy Garland, Gene Kelly, and Shirley Temple, became a Senator, representing the State of California from 1965 until 1971. Ronald Reagan and Arnold Schwarzenegger, fellow California film personalities, have since followed in George Murphy's nimble footsteps.

Nowadays, we not only appoint celebrities as our politicians, but we authorise our celebrities to become political commentators. One need only consider the enormous amount of press coverage allotted, for instance, to the British-born Hollywood film star Jude Law, speaking about his views on the Taliban (cf. Hyde, 2009; Payne, 2009).

The adoration of celebrities has become so ubiquitous that even those who have already achieved celebrity status still crave contact, nonetheless, with other well-known people. I once arranged an initial psychotherapy session with a noted public figure, but this person, whom I shall call "Z", did not arrive at the appointed time. Some fifteen minutes into the session, Z pressed the buzzer at my office and entered my consulting room, fully penitent for having kept me waiting. Naively, I had assumed that Z might have had difficulty finding my building but, in fact, Z confessed that en route to the consultation, he had passed a fellow celebrity, one far *less* famous than Z, in fact, but one whom Z had long adored nonetheless, and Z then spent fully one quarter of an hour following this other celebrity down the street, stalker-like and thoroughly entranced.

Even Noël Coward succumbed to the lure of celebrities greater than himself. When the four Beatles received their M.B.E. [Member of the Most Excellent Order of the British Empire] awards, Coward (1965a, p. 602) complained about their "talentless but considerable contributions to the Exchequer". Some two weeks later, Coward (1965b, p. 602) forced himself to attend a Beatles concert, which he described as "just one long, ear-splitting din", and he experienced the audience as "a mass masturbation orgy" (Coward, 1965b, p. 602). The composer and dramatist, who had spent his entire lifetime in show business, further opined,

> To realize that the majority of the modern adolescent world goes ritualistically mad over those four innocuous, rather silly-looking young men is a disturbing thought. Perhaps we are whirling more swiftly into extinction than we know. Personally I should have liked to take some of those squealing young maniacs and cracked their heads together. [Coward, 1965b, pp. 602–603]

Yet in spite of his odium for the Beatles and their fans, Coward insisted on an audience with the Liverpudlian singers afterwards, and, upon greeting Paul McCartney, the elderly Coward lied through gritted teeth and told the moppet-haired Beatle how much he had enjoyed the performance. Afterwards, he wrote in his private diary, perhaps more truthfully: "the message I would have liked to send them was that they were bad-mannered little shits" (Coward, 1965b, p. 602).

In view of the mass impact of celebrification, it seems that Britons even require the attendance of celebrities at our funerals. Few among us will not have seen the television coverage of the heart-wrenching service at London's Westminster Abbey for Diana, Princess of Wales, in 1997. In addition to members of her family and heads of state, the guest list also included Tom Cruise, Tom Hanks, Elton John, Luciano Pavarotti, and Steven Spielberg.

Celebrity also infuses our sexual fantasy life, perhaps quite unsurprisingly so. In my own work as Principal Investigator for the British Sexual Fantasy Research Project, conducted over many years, I surveyed more than 25,000 British and American adult sexual fantasies. As part of the research, I asked participants whether they had ever experienced either masturbatory fantasies or coital fantasies about celebrities, and I discovered that approximately 25% of British adult participants will have had an orgasm while imagining a sexual scenario with a film star, pop star, television star, or sports star, with young people between the ages of 18 and 24 years being three times more likely to do so than the over-sixties.

The British-based research participants reported the following fantasies about celebrities, in descending order of preference: straight sex, oral sex, visual arousal, romantic scenes, fetishistic scenes, sadomasochism, group sex, submission to celebrities, anal sex, domination of celebrities, sex in public/exhibitionism, and extreme sexual violence (Kahr, 2007a; cf. Kahr, 2008). Indeed, one of the interviewees in my research study, an elderly male scientist, told me that he could reach orgasm *only* by fantasising that the Swedish monarch had presented him with a Nobel Prize. Solely through the acquisition of imaginary scientific fame could this gentleman achieve full sexual satisfaction.

We have become so preoccupied with celebrities that we even pay good money to stare at wax representations of them, as evidenced by the popularity of Madame Tussauds wax-work museum, with headquarters in London and branches in many additional locations, including Hollywood, California; Las Vegas, Nevada; Nashville, Tennessee; New York City, New York; Washington, D.C., not to mention Amsterdam, Bangkok, Beijing, Berlin, Hong Kong, Istanbul, New Delhi, Prague, Shanghai, Sydney, and Vienna. At least Madame Tussauds has based its waxworks on *real* celebrities still living, or on those who had once lived. Sometimes, we even worship celebrities who never existed *at all*.

In the early 1930s, the witty American songwriter Cole Porter created a fictitious *parvenu* couple from Tulsa, Oklahoma, called "Mr. and Mrs. S. Beech Fitch",[10] about whom he spoke so frequently that newspapers eventually published reports of their comings and goings. One article claimed that the Fitches would be staying with Cole Porter and his wife Linda Porter in Konigsvilla in Carlsbad, and thereafter would be the guests of notable socialites, such as Count Laszlo Szechenyi in Hungary, as well as Countess Emanuela Potocka in Poland and the Marquis Hélie de Talleyrand-Périgord in Rome and, ultimately, would have an audience with Pope Pius XI (Anonymous, n.d.). Famed newspaper columnists Walter Winchell and, also, Maury Paul, better known as "Cholly Knickerbocker", eventually exposed the scandal, and Porter subsequently immortalised the fictitious celebrity couple in an eponymous song "Mister and Missus Fitch" (Porter, c. 1931), which eventually appeared in the composer's 1932

Broadway musical *The Gay Divorce*, starring Fred Astaire. The myth of the Fitches has remained firmly fixed in popular consciousness, and the couple even became the focus of a Broadway play in 2010, *Mr. and Mrs. Fitch*, about a pair of gossip columnists, written by Douglas Carter Beane.

In 1930, the British novelist Evelyn Waugh (1930) spoofed this trend for admiring fictitious celebrities in his satire *Vile Bodies*. When the feckless protagonist "Adam Fenwick-Symes" succeeded to the post of "Mr Chatterbox" on the *Daily Excess* newspaper, he quickly invented a series of *faux* celebrities to fill his column, such as "Provna", the Polish sculptor. Eventually, various pieces of art attributed to the elusive "Provna", made uniquely from cork, vulcanite, and steel, began to appear in Bond Street galleries! With his literary finesse, Waugh captured brilliantly the way in which we succumb to the seductive allure of celebrity, even when built upon the very flimsiest of foundations.

We not only become excited by "real" celebrities and, also, by fictional or waxwork celebrities, but it seems that even our celestial gods and goddesses must become media personalities. In Marie Phillips's (2007) novel *Gods Behaving Badly*, about ancient Greek deities living in modern-day North London, the character of "Apollo", now cast as a psychic, has his own television show, *Apollo's Oracle*, as well as an agent who handles his business deals. Indeed, even though Apollo has the opportunity to have sexual intercourse with "Aphrodite", the most beautiful woman in creation, he prefers to indulge instead in private sexual fantasies about Catherine Zeta-Jones while penetrating Aphrodite, wishing that the Greek goddess had a Welsh accent. As art imitates life, Phillips's novel eventually became an eponymous movie, which premiered at the Rome Film Festival in 2013.

In 2003, Dr John Maltby, a psychologist at the University of Leicester, even identified a so-called "Celebrity Worship Syndrome", noting that approximately one-third of the British population suffers from this constellation of obsessive symptoms (cf. Chapman, 2003).

In fact, failure to be a celebrity has even become a crime. On 23 March 2003, the American actor Steve Martin, while hosting The 75th Annual Academy Awards, cried out in mock horror to the crowd of stars, "Oh, I'm sorry, I thought I saw a non-celebrity."

The profusion of celebrity culture has, at long last, begun to distress and irritate people, and public commentators have criticised this phenomenon quite bluntly. The broadcaster Jeremy Vine (2017, p. 117) issued a clarion call, published in the *Radio Times*, recommending that the current crop of celebrities should be culled by 70%, and that in future, in order to be a celebrity, one would need a special permit. Vine insisted, "Magazines—even this one—would not be allowed to feature prominent photos of unlicensed people, or they would face severe fines. This ambitious scheme would do nothing short of rationing the amount of fame, and would make it far more likely that we would produce great artists like David Bowie."

As we have mentioned, Noël Coward had assumed that, "we are whirling more swiftly into extinction than we know", and he attributed the demise of modern civilisation to the Beatles. Indeed, each of us assumes that the younger generation should be held entirely responsible for the rise of crass celebrity culture. After all, our parents and grandparents never salivated over daily doses of gossip about unfaithful golf professionals, such as Tiger Woods, or cuckolded Hollywood actresses, such as Sandra Bullock. Or did they? Can we dismiss our preoccupation with famous people as an exclusively modern symptom? Can we institute a legal ban against celebrities? Or might we discover that the fetishisation of celebrity has actually occupied an important role in our psychological landscape for many centuries? Perhaps we harbour a strong and long-standing unconscious need for such persons in our otherwise humdrum lives.

THREE

"I woke up the next morning and found myself famous": towards a history of notoriety

He became a celebrity; he became at last a great man.

Lytton Strachey on Dr Thomas Arnold
[Strachey, 1918, p. 208]

I hope that, in the preceding chapters, I have begun to dispel the prevailing myth that all celebrities suffer from exhibitionism and grandiosity. Although certain famous people *do*, indeed, struggle with these psychodynamics, I would argue that a much greater intrapsychic conflict exists in the minds of the *audience*—the "civilians", as model and actress Elizabeth Hurley calls us—those of us who pay good money to sustain the fame industry.

I now wish to scotch a second myth—namely, that the so-called Celebrity Worship Syndrome represents a thoroughly *modern* phenomenon and an indication that our culture has begun to deteriorate in an invidious manner, especially in the wake of the proliferation of so-called "reality television" programmes (cf. Inglis, 2010). This could not be further from the truth, as even the most perfunctory scrutiny of historical data reveals that the preoccupation with fame and celebrity has featured as an integral part of human psychological life for thousands of years, if not longer. Let us examine merely a few historical landmarks.

According to Professor Leo Braudy (1986), a distinguished American littérateur and cultural historian at the University of Southern California in Los Angeles, fame has a long history, dating back at least to the time of Alexander the Great, who represents, for Braudy, the first celebrity, in view of Alexander's sustained campaign to preserve his own image on coins and in statuary.

But one can readily find substantial references to a preoccupation with fame long before the reign of Alexander. In ancient Greece, Homer spoke of the concept of "*kleos aphthiton*" ["imperishable fame"] in the *Iliad*. Furthermore, in his epic poem the *Aeneid* (*Book X*, 468), the ancient Roman author Publius Vergilius Maro, better known as Virgil, enshrined the notion of "*famam extendere factis*" ["to extend fame by deeds"]. Other classical writers who came to engage with this subject have included Herodotus and Hesiod, as well as Plutarch and Xenophon (Boitani, 1984).

The Middle Ages also brim with references to the subject—unsurprisingly so, in view of the heightened Christian concern with the question of the afterlife and whether one will be remembered in the wake of one's death. For instance, in his late-fourteenth-century poem "Hous of Fame",[11] Geoffrey Chaucer (c. 1379–1380, p. 244) wrote about "how hit was writen ful of names, / Of folks that hadden grete fames" (cf. Delany, 1972).

As the centuries have unfolded, one could, of course, refer to literally hundreds of historical examples of people seeking notoriety. Even the late-fifteenth-century Cornish blacksmith, Mighell Ioseph (later known as Michael Joseph an Gof)—who stirred rebellion, protesting against King Henry

VII's levy of taxes in order to fight the Scots—proclaimed, while en route to his execution, that, "he should haue a name perpetual and a fame permanēt and immortal"[12] (Hall, 1548, p. 479).

The Tudors also boasted a crop of overnight celebrities, notably three ostensibly "holy maidens", such as the Holy Maid of Leominster, who boasted that she could survive on nothing more than daily communion and, consequently, became a "superstar" during the reign of Henry VII, attracting large crowds, until the king's mother, Lady Margaret Beaufort, the Countess of Richmond and Derby, unmasked the Leominster maid as a fraud who ate several meals daily, assisted by a deceptive curate (Rex, 1993). Another woman, the Holy Maid of Ipswich, who flourished in 1516, claimed to be cured, miraculously, of epilepsy, as did Elizabeth Barton, the Holy Maid of Kent, who prophesied her own recovery from epilepsy on Annunciation Day (Rex, 1993). These Tudor religious performers became instant sensations, and one suspects that had they lived several centuries later, they would, no doubt, have launched their own Twitter campaigns. Even Henry VIII himself, already one of the most famous men in the world and certainly the most notorious in England during the sixteenth century, prompted William Blount, Lord Mountjoy (Blount, 1509, p. 450),[13] to write to Desiderius Erasmus, the distinguished man of letters, "Noster Rex non aurum, non gemmas, non metalla, sed virtutem, sed gloriam, sed aeternitatem concupiscit." ["Our King's heart is set not upon gold, or jewels, or mines of ore, but upon virtue, reputation, and eternal fame."]

The Elizabethans also pursued notoriety with considerable fervour. In his play *As You Like It*, written circa 1599–1600, William Shakespeare pontificated about the dangers of young men "Seeking the bubble reputation" (Act II, Scene vii, 152), as part of the memorable "All the world's a stage" speech, delivered by the melancholy character "Jaques". In Shakespeare's later play, *Troilus and Cressida*, penned circa 1602, and first published under the title *The Famous Hiſtorie of Troylus and Creſſeid*, the character of "Achilles" exclaims, "I see my reputation is at stake / My fame is shrowdly gor'd" (Act III, Scene iii, 227).

The paintings of the Elizabethan period, like its drama, brim with references to the subject of renown. The figure of "Fame", an allegorical image, appears in the memorial portrait of Sir Henry Unton, completed circa 1596, which one can view at London's National Portrait Gallery (NPG 710) (cf. Strong, 1977). Similarly, a reference to fame can be observed, almost as a warning, on the oil painting of the Elizabethan poet Sir Philip Sidney, also preserved in the National Portrait Gallery (NPG 2096), which bears the inscription "CAETERA FAMA", which might be translated as "All the rest is fame". Such a message suggests that only the portrait reveals the true man, and that anything else should be construed as little more than fame or rumour. Indeed, Sidney's legacy inspired John Addington Symonds (1886, p. 1), the nineteenth-century man of letters, to opine that,

> The real difficulty of painting an adequate portrait of Sidney at the present time is that his renown transcends his actual achievement. Neither his poetry nor his prose, nor what is known about his action, quite explains the singular celebrity which he enjoyed in his own life, and the fame which has attended his memory with almost undimmed lustre through three centuries.

Indeed, across the early modern period, many pursued fame through the creation of tombs, brasses, and other types of funerary art as a means of striving for immortality. Sir Thomas

Elyot (1531, p. 265), the noted English scholar, referred to this phenomenon as the quest for "perpetuall memory", a privilege that would be enjoyed by those in recognition of "the iuste rewarde of their vertue"[14] (Elyot, 1531, p. 265).

By the mid-eighteenth century, the English novelist Laurence Sterne, best remembered as the author of *The Life and Opinions of Tristram Shandy, Gentleman*, explained, in a letter to an unknown correspondent, dated 30 January 1760, that he had embarked upon writing "not to be *fed*, but to be *famous*" (Sterne, 1760, p. 22). Contemporaneously, the French philosopher and *encyclopédiste* Denis Diderot and the sculptor Étienne Maurice Falconet engaged in a famous debate, the "*dispute sur la postérité*"—the dispute about posterity—arguing whether it would be preferable to strive for fame in one's lifetime or, by contrast, to become renowned after one's death (Diderot, 1765–1767). Strikingly, Diderot (1766/1831, p. 218) emphasised that, "*Tant de grands noms oubliés! tant de grands hommes dont les ouvrages sont perdus ou détruits!*" ["So many great names forgotten! so many great men whose works are lost or destroyed!"]. Falconet, who advocated the former position—pre-mortem celebrity—published their correspondence and became quite famous at the time, though his name has since plummeted into obscurity, whereas Diderot, who endorsed the latter position—post-mortem fame—has become a legendary figure in the pantheon of great philosophers.

Fame even penetrated the eighteenth-century prison system. During the *Règne de la Terreur* in France, infamous penal institutions such as the Conciergerie in Paris offered special provision for wealthy so-called celebrity prisoners, who awaited their executions by guillotine in private cells fitted with a small cot and a bed. The more ordinary prisoners, by contrast, known as the "*pailleux*" (Bijaoui, 1996, p. 30) [i.e., those who slept on straw], had to share vermin-infested cells.

The lust for fame flourished throughout the nineteenth century as well. For instance, in 1812, the appearance of the first section of the narrative poem *Childe Harold's Pilgrim-age*, written by George Gordon, Lord Byron, exerted such an impact that Thomas Moore (1833, p. 255), who became Byron's biographer, remarked, "the impression which it produced upon the public was as instantaneous as it has proved deep and lasting", and that, "The effect was, accordingly, electric;—his fame had not to wait for any of the ordinary gradations, but seemed to spring up, like the palace of a fairy tale, in a night" (Moore, 1833, p. 258). Indeed, Lord Byron himself exclaimed, "I awoke one morning and found myself famous" (quoted in Moore, 1833, p. 258).

The publication of *Childe Harold's Pilgrimage* and the cap-tivating personality of the poet himself unleashed a veritable flood of "Byromania" (MacCarthy, 2002, p. 160; cf. Moore, 1838; Quennell, 1935). Byron's observation about overnight fame became sufficiently well known among men of letters—so much so that composer Arthur Sullivan, the future collab-orator of William Schwenk Gilbert, found himself deploying much the same phrase when, after having conducted a perfor-mance of his first seminal musical composition, *The Tempest*, at London's Crystal Palace on 5 April 1862, noted: "It is no exaggeration to say that I woke up the next morning and found myself famous" (quoted in Baily, 1973, p. 17).

In the mid-nineteenth century, Emily Dickinson wrote an undated poem about the subject of celebrity. The unti-tled fragment reads as follows: "Fame is a bee. / It has a song— / It has a sting— / Ah, too, it has a wing." And in 1878, the year in which the social-climbing Oscar Wilde left the University of Oxford, he wrote to his friend David

Hunter-Blair: "I won't be a dried-up Oxford don, anyhow. I'll be a poet, a writer, a dramatist. Somehow or other I'll be famous" (quoted in Von Eckardt, Gilman, and Chamberlin, 1987, p. 1; cf. Ellmann, 1987).

With the dawning of the twentieth century, fame and celebrity fairly exploded, much assisted by the new media, especially motion pictures. In the era of silent films, stars such as Mary Pickford and Douglas Fairbanks became the new gods of the Western world. According to the *American Magazine* of May 1918, Mary Pickford received more letters daily than did President Woodrow Wilson (Barbas, 2001). Indeed, when Miss Pickford divorced Mr Fairbanks in 1935, long after the acme of her career, the couple's separation made front-page news.

Few film stars captured the imagination of the general public quite as much as Rudolph Valentino. And when this silent screen icon died in 1926 at the premature age of 31 years from peritonitis and pleuritis, fans became hysterical with grief. Tens of thousands of worshippers cluttered the streets outside the funeral parlour in New York City, causing so much disruption that mounted police had to intervene, trampling one female bystander in the process. Even Benito Mussolini had a commemorative wreath sent to honour the great film star (Botham, 2002). In faraway London, England, a young woman called Peggy Scott, inconsolable at the news of Valentino's death, penned a desperate note: "I am only a little butterfly made for sunshine and I cannot stand loneliness and shadow" (quoted in Barbas, 2001, p. 169). Miss Scott then promptly swallowed a bottle of poison and died. The coverage of Valentino's funeral proved so tremendous that it completely eclipsed the death of Charles Eliot, President of Harvard University, who passed away on the day of Valentino's burial, thus provoking outrage among academics.

Throughout the 1920s and 1930s, Americans, in particular, not only idolised celebrities but, also, yearned to emulate them, desperate to launch their own 1920s-style *Pop Idol*-like careers. In 1921, the 14-year-old Clara Gordon Bow of Bay Ridge, in Brooklyn, New York, borrowed $1 for a photo session so that she could enter the "Fame and Fortune Contest" sponsored by such magazines as *Motion Picture*, *Motion Picture Classic*, and *Shadowland* (Stenn, 1988). As a result of the competition, Miss Bow catapulted to stardom and then went on to feature in the 1927 film *It*, playing the role of "Betty Lou", a shop girl on the rise—yet another example of art imitating life.

Merton of the Movies, released in 1924, chronicled one man's journey to become an actor. This motion picture served as a template for many others that followed, such as Harold Lloyd's 1932 film, *Movie Crazy*, which portrayed a hapless comic who takes the picture industry by storm; and Constance Bennett's 1932 movie *What Price Hollywood?*, which depicted a Brown Derby waitress called "Mary Evans" who hoped to launch a celebrity career; and, additionally, *Make Me a Star*, also released in 1932, the first of several remakes of *Merton of the Movies*. In the 1937 film *Hollywood Hotel*, the saxophonist "Ronnie Bowers"—played by the popular heartthrob Dick Powell—has signed a ten-week contract with Miracle Pictures. Upon his arrival in Hollywood, the assembled crowd serenades him with the sensational popular song "Hooray for Hollywood", whose lyrics offer the promise that "any office boy or young mechanic can be a panic".

Byronic notions of overnight fame impacted not only upon the movies but, also, upon the theatre. The American writer Ben Hecht described Broadway songsmith and entrepreneur Billy Rose, perhaps best remembered as the co-lyricist of the 1933 song "It's Only a Paper Moon", as a "fame hunter" (quoted in Marx and Clayton, 1976, p. 177) who feared "waking in the morning and, like an inverse Byron, finding himself unknown" (quoted in Marx and Clayton, 1976, p. 177).

Some craved recognition through the cinema, but others did so more modestly by participating in local and national talent competitions, first on radio and then on television, such as the *Major Bowes Amateur Hour*, *The Original Amateur Hour*, and, eventually, *Star Search*.

For those who had no discernible singing talent or screen presence, one could nevertheless still *purchase* a piece of symbolic celebrity. Indeed, the American actress Joan Crawford caused an enormous sensation in the 1932 film *Letty Lynton* by wearing fashion designer Adrian's fetching dress with puffy, ruffled shoulders; and, in consequence, a chain of stores called Cinema Shop promptly manufactured and sold some 500,000 copies of this gown, as innumerable American women wished to look exactly like Miss Crawford. The *Letty Lynton* dress became extremely iconic, and Adrian claimed that this episode ensured the future of his career as a celebrity fashion designer (Chierichetti, 1976). Similarly, in the 1930s virtually every American girl craved Shirley Temple artefacts and memorabilia, consequently forcing parents to purchase Shirley Temple dresses, hats, underwear, dolls, soap, and milk mugs (Scherman, 1975). Millions craved fame, and anyone who yearned for press attention would be known, colloquially, as a "lens louse" (quoted in Maxwell, 1954, p. 205).

Everyone simply *had* to become famous in Depression-era America. In the 1933 blockbuster musical film *42ⁿᵈ Street*, the character of the director "Julian Marsh", portrayed by Warner Baxter, pleads with understudy-turned-leading lady "Peggy Sawyer", played by Ruby Keeler: "Sawyer, you're going out a youngster, but you've *got* to come back a star." This oft-quoted line of dialogue became the veritable *cri de coeur* for 1930s

America, underscoring that celebrity had now become no longer an *option* but, rather, a *necessity*.

It would be naïve to assume that during the early twentieth century only the Americans worshipped the pursuit of fame. Contrary to popular opinion, Great Britain did not remain immune to this seemingly crass American bid for overnight stardom. In 1939, a British film called *Let's Be Famous* appeared on local screens, about an Irish singer who yearns for stardom and who ends up featured on a quiz programme. The movie showcased Sonnie Hale, a well-known personality of British stage and screen (once married to fellow performer Evelyn Laye, and then to Jessie Matthews), as well as Betty Driver, who would subsequently appear for many years on the popular television soap opera *Coronation Street*.

Celebrity culture became so alluring that even those who had already achieved public recognition for their exploits yearned to experiment with even higher levels of fame and notoriety. Indeed, in the summer of 1927, the so-called "Bright Young Things"—London's smart set of revellers, frequently lampooned by Evelyn Waugh—decided to host an "Impersonation Party" (Lancaster, 1968, p. 229), also known as the "'Living Celebrity' party" (Hoare, 1990, p. 83), at the home of Captain Neil McEachran on Brook Street, in Central London. On that occasion, each of these already proven social celebrities endeavoured to outdo themselves by dressing up as *other* celebrities. In particular, the Honourable Stephen Tennant, a well-known aristocratic dilettante of the period, garnered much publicity for his impersonation of Queen Marie of Roumania, sporting a high-necked Edwardian white silk dress, with gloves, pearls, as well as an elaborate hair style (Hoare, 1990; cf. Taylor, 2007).

One could provide an endless stream of comparable instances of the search for fame in both American and British culture and, also, in other countries, but I hope that these aforementioned instances will suffice to demonstrate the long-standing interest in celebritisation. This all too brief "history" of fame and celebrity should provide at least an inkling that such notions have preoccupied human beings for century upon century and that, perhaps, such an obsession indicates what an important role fame has long occupied in our inner world. We may come to discover, in fact, that the lust for fame represents not only an expression of pathological narcissism but, also, perhaps, a very basic human need to be seen.

FOUR

"Mama getting out of the bathtub in the nude": the roots of celebrification

. . . a thing that worldly men desire greatly that their fame might last long after them here upon earth.

Sir John Clanvowe, fourteenth century
[Quoted in Thomas, 2009, p. 235]

Let us pause for a moment to recapitulate. What have we learned thus far? First of all, the search for celebrity should be regarded as by no means a new phenomenon sparked off by the much-publicised genre of entertainment programmes known as "reality television". In truth, the surge to become famous has constituted a crucial part of our cultural history across the centuries. But in the wake of Freudianism, perhaps we have begun to discover that the desire to generate celebrities whom we can idolise, idealise, and denigrate might well lie at the very heart of human nature. Second of all, in our lust to create stars or to become stars, we have neglected the role of the *audience*, perhaps by far the larger component in the complex marital relationship between those who allow themselves to be watched and those who do the watching.

But how have we reached a point in human history in which celebrities of every ilk have come to dominate our consciousness and, perhaps, our unconsciousness in such a pervasive and arguably alarming fashion? Clive James (1993), the distinguished broadcaster and cultural commentator, has wondered how, for instance, Yoko Ono could become the most famous and best-recognised Japanese person alive, simply by virtue of having married a very well-known man, namely, the singer and songwriter John Lennon.

Professor Leo Braudy (1986, p. 17) noted that one could characterise fame as "a subject about which everyone has something to say". Indeed, we have no shortage of superficial theories that attempt to explain the perseverance of the phenomena of celebrity and fame. Some have argued that modern celebrity culture has developed as one of the legacies of the late-nineteenth-century rise of universal literacy and the growing success of the press and, ultimately, of radio, film, and television in establishing celebrities as internationally recognisable and bankable commodities, capable of generating income for capitalistic bureaucrats. This strikes me as rather a reasonable theory. Others have suggested that the declining popularity of organised world religions, as well as the collapse of the omnipotent European Royal houses (e.g., the Habsburgs, the Hohenzollerns, the Romanovs, and the Wittelsbachs) has created, in public consciousness, a void once filled by princes, and that our film stars and pop stars and sporting stars have become the new potentates at whose feet we worship. Did not football hero David Beckham and his "Spice Girl" spouse Victoria Adams Beckham sit, famously, on *faux* thrones, at the fifteenth-century Luttrellstown Castle, on the outskirts of Dublin, in Ireland, at their much-publicised wedding celebrations in 1999? This, too, strikes me as rather a good theory—namely, that stars have become the new crowned heads.

But although the rise of the media, and the increase in urbanisation, and the fall of the monarchy, as well as the growing de-Christianisation of the Western world, have all provided us with an historico-political backdrop to the proliferation of celebrity culture, one wonders whether modern depth psychology might have any contribution to make to the study of this perennially engaging polemic? After all, Sigmund Freud, the greatest psychoanalytic theoretician of all time, had flourished during that era when silent films emerged as the most popular form of entertainment, and he witnessed these developments at first hand.

Although we have referred to some of Freud's *aperçus* on fame in the introductory chapter to this text, we regret that he never wrote about fame and celebrity in a sustained or systematic manner. I would argue that we can learn most, perhaps, about the unconscious psychodynamics of fame from Freud's (1909a) observations, originally published in German as a short, untitled insert in a book written by Otto Rank (1909), *Der Mythus von der Geburt des Helden: Versuch einer psychologischen Mythendeutung* [*The Myth of the Birth of the Hero: A Psychological Interpretation of Mythology* (Rank, 1914)]. These remarks ultimately appeared in English translation, known as "Family Romances" (Freud, 1909b, 1909c). In this modest communication, Freud noted a widespread phenomenon among children—namely, the tendency to imagine oneself in fantasy *not* as the child of Herr X and Frau X but, rather, as the son or daughter of a member of the aristocracy. According to Freud (1909c, p. 238), these daydreams and imaginings serve as "the fulfilment of wishes"[15] and as "a correction of actual life"[16] (Freud, 1909c, p. 238). In other words, "the child's

53

imagination becomes engaged in the task of getting free from the parents of whom he now has a low opinion and of replacing them by others, who, as a rule, are of higher social standing"[17] (Freud, 1909c, pp. 238–239). Sigmund Freud referred to this phenomenon as the "family romance"[18] (cf. Kahr, 2002c).

Who among us has not harboured a fantasy of living in a palace, with servants to wait on our every need? And when we gawp at the luxurious photographs of wealthy people in *Hello!* magazine, do we not do so, at least in part, to indulge a private fantasy that, one day, we might also come to own a comparable estate?

Although intended only as a brief *pièce d'occasion*, Freud's short communication on the family romance provides an important clue to the psychology of celebrity culture. Regrettably, Freud wrote no further about this phenomenon in any great detail. Among his immediate followers, only the English psychoanalyst, child psychiatrist, and paediatrician Dr Donald Winnicott elaborated upon the importance of celebrity. Indeed, in his little-quoted membership paper on "The Manic Defence", presented to the British Psycho-Analytical Society in 1935, Winnicott made a passing and completely overlooked comment about the preoccupation with the Court Circular published in stolid newspapers such as *The Times*, which provided an itinerary of the comings and goings of the senior members of the Royal Family. As Winnicott (1935, p. 131) observed, "in order to account for the existence of the Court and Personal column of our newspapers we must postulate a general need for reassurance against ideas of illness and death in the Royal Family and among the aristocracy; such reassurance can be given by reliable publication of facts." He added, further, that,

"In these Court and Personal columns the movements of the aristocracy are reported and predicted, and here can be seen in thin disguise the omnipotent control of personages who stand for internal objects" (Winnicott, 1935, p. 131). Although I have seen references to this paper in the psychoanalytic literature, I can recall no articles or books which have referred specifically to Winnicott's particular observations about royalty and the aristocracy, with the exception of a fleeting mention offered by Dr Wilfred Bion (1961) in his book on groups.

Winnicott's short essay—his very first official psychoanalytic paper, in fact, and one that would not be published until more than twenty-two years after its first presentation—contains many important nuggets that will help us to create a psychological theory about our obsession with celebrity culture. First of all, Winnicott posited that famous people—in this case, the Royal family and other aristocrats—become symbolic substitutes in our minds for early parental figures. Second of all, Winnicott noted that we, as citizens, seem to have a need to keep tabs on the whereabouts of these parental figures, reassuring ourselves that they have not died. After all, do we not refer to the eldest female in the Royal Family as the "Queen *Mother*", and does the monarch not always keep the flag flying at Buckingham Palace to indicate his or her presence or absence? (cf. Winnicott, 1970). In other words, scouring the Court Circular, or *Hello!* magazine, or internet fan sites allows us to identify the whereabouts of our symbolically venerated and, often, parentified celebrities, and in doing so, we both delight in the fact that they have not yet died, and we take pleasure, further, in the fact that we gain some degree of surreptitious control over them, knowing all about their private lives.

How many of us, in babyhood, suffered acute anxieties when our mother disappeared for a certain period of time and left us in a state of terror, not knowing whether she would ever return? Fortunately, as we develop in age and capacity, we begin to conquer these primitive terrors. Our ever-growing cognitive and motoric abilities enable us to roam about the house in search of our mothers; and our increased linguistic skills permit us to understand that when our mother explains that she must leave the room for a few minutes, we know that she has not died. Winnicott's observations about the need of the general newspaper-reading public to be reassured through the Court Circular provide helpful, yet neglected, insights into our preoccupation with celebrities as parental substitutes and with celebrities as caregivers whom we track and whom we yearn to control.

Although few commentators have remarked upon this fact, Winnicott's 1935 paper on "The Manic Defence" actually contains the kernels of one of his most important contributions to psychoanalysis, one that he would not publish until 1969, nearly thirty-five years later, namely, that of "The Use of an Object", a much better known paper, yet one still not fully appreciated by the psychoanalytic community at large. In this essay, originally delivered before the New York Psychoanalytic Society in 1968, Winnicott (1969) proposed that the dedicated psychoanalyst must allow himself or herself to be deployed by the patient as an object, and that this experience might include a ruthless use of the analyst as a vehicle for the discharge of unneutralised, murderous rage. According to the testimony of Dr Robert Langs (2002), then a young American psychiatrist (and subsequently a venerable psychoanalyst) who heard Winnicott lecture in New York in the 1960s, that particular paper proved to be quite shocking, because it seemed to undermine the traditional power and authority of the psychoanalyst and turned the analyst into a figure who might be abused, violating the stereotype of the analyst as an icon of supreme wisdom, who dedicated his or her time solely to the interpretation of the patient's unconscious mind in a straightforward manner. Above all, Winnicott's schematisation underscored the truly reciprocal, interactional nature of the psychoanalytic process, wherein the psychologies of both parties play a strong role—an observation that, according to Langs, violated the more medicalised post-World War-II notion of the psychoanalyst as a neutral person who did nothing but cure the patient's madness.

Winnicott's concept of "The Use of an Object" certainly merits our ongoing consideration. Happily, we can draw upon his idea in this context of the celebrity as an "object" used by a "fan". Thus, a fan who indulges in a sexual fantasy about a celebrity or vilifies a celebrity in conversation has engaged in the use of that famous person as an object for the fulfilment of certain unconscious needs. Likewise, celebrities have the capacity to use fans as objects as well—for instance, when a celebrity performs in front of a large audience in order to be seen, heard, and, indeed, paid, said celebrity has used the fan or fans as objects who serve a variety of very basic needs.

The noted film icon Clark Gable, though certainly not a psychoanalyst, knew only too well about this mutual interactional process that unfolds between stars and their audiences. After Thelma Todd, a minor Hollywood film actress who starred opposite the Marx Brothers in *Monkey Business* and *Horse Feathers*, died under mysterious circumstances from carbon monoxide poisoning in 1935, Clark Gable shared his observations on the tragedy with the younger actor David

Niven. Gable expounded, "Thelma didn't read the small print" (quoted in Niven, 1975, p. 34). When Niven queried this remark, Gable explained further,

> Yes. We all have a contract with the public—in us they see themselves or what they would like to be. On the screen and in our private lives, we are the standards by which they measure their own ideals of everything—sex, guts, humour, stupidity, cowardice, crumminess—you name it. They love to put us on a pedestal and worship us and form fan clubs and write thousands of letters telling us how great we are. But *they've* read the small print, and most of *us* haven't—they expect us to pay the price for it all . . . we have to get it in the end! So, when we get knocked off by gangsters, like Thelma did, or get hooked on booze or dope or get ourselves thrown out of the business because of scandals or because we just get old, that's the payoff and the public feels satisfied. Yeah, it's a good idea to read that small print. [Quoted in Niven, 1975, pp. 34–35]

Although Clark Gable did not offer his observation in the language of Freudian metapsychology, he actually came extremely close to having done so, anticipating Winnicott's more elaborated viewpoint with good horse sense. Whether we espouse Gable's ideas about the unwritten contract between the star and the fans, or whether we endorse Winnicott's notion that exalted personages become internal objects whom we must track in order to minimise abandonment anxiety or into whom we must discharge death wishes in order to neutralise our own primitive hatred, both the homespun version and the psychoanalytically sophisticated encapsulation provide us with important building blocks in terms of our construction of a more comprehensive theory of celebrity.

In my researches, I have discovered only one other small psychoanalytic contribution of immediate value for the study of celebrity, namely a remark made, *en passant*, in 1937, by the distinguished American psychiatrist and psychoanalyst Dr Karl Menninger, of Topeka, Kansas, after he had visited the plush Vendôme restaurant on Hollywood's Sunset Boulevard, an eatery often frequented by movie stars. Reporting on his experiences, Dr Menninger (1937, p. 235) boasted that he had seen several film personalities "at close range". He also explained that, "Trying to see these movie stars in the flesh is a game here and seems to be related to the impulse to see Mama getting out of the bathtub in the nude. Anyway they all do it and we follow suit" (Menninger, 1937, p. 235).

Menninger's letter deserves our interest for at least two reasons. First of all, he has drawn successfully upon early Freudian theories of the so-called "Urszene" (Freud, 1918a, p. 617) or "primal scene" (Freud, 1918b, p. 39), namely, the wish of the young infant to enter the parental bedroom to avoid painful feelings of exclusion. Menninger had appreciated that the wish to stare at celebrities and to learn about their private lives represents a sublimation of this quite primitive, archaic impulse to see our parents *in flagrante*. And yet, interestingly, in spite of Menninger's own psychoanalytic training, he still found himself quite compelled by a deep-seated voyeuristic urge to gawp along with all the other tourists from Kansas and elsewhere ("Anyway they all do it and we follow suit"), as though he had lost all sense of discernment or agency. So, the wish to learn about the private lives of celebrities may, indeed, represent something extremely fundamental in human nature.

Apart from these brief, though seminal, contributions from Sigmund Freud, Donald Winnicott, and Karl Menninger, the psychoanalytic literature on celebrity culture remains rather sparse. Most of the other publications on this subject tend to be of the more boastful variety, in which distinguished psychoanalysts have written about their travails in treating the beautiful, the wealthy, and the famous (e.g., Wahl, 1974,

1975a, 1975b; Greenson, 1978; Farber and Green, 1993; cf. Feldman, 1975; Garma, 1975; Gilliland, 1975; Heimann, 1975; Miller, 1975; Saul, 1975). Thus, the field remains still quite wide open for further conceptualisation and understanding of the ways in which psychoanalytic ideas can enlighten us about vital cultural phenomena (cf. Richards, 1984, 2014; Bainbridge and Yates, 2007; Bainbridge, 2014; MacRury and Rustin, 2014; Yates, 2014a, 2014b, 2015).

FIVE

"Drag the sublime into the mud": towards a more comprehensive theory of celebrity

No one writes to achieve fame, which anyhow is a very transitory matter, or the illusion of immortality. Surely we write first of all to satisfy something within ourselves, not for other people.

Professor Sigmund Freud, personal communication
to Princesse Marie Bonaparte, 1925
[Freud, 1925, p. 397]

Having benefited enormously from the foundation stones laid by Freud and his followers, I shall now elaborate a more integrated and comprehensive theory, which, I trust, will endeavour to explain our deep-seated, never-ending preoccupation with fame and celebrity, encompassing both our very human wish to become famous ourselves and our desire to align ourselves with those who have already done so. I shall draw not only upon a century of psychoanalytic thinking, both classical and modern, but, also, upon my own experiences as a clinician who has worked with those who have achieved fame and those who have aspired to fame, as well as those who purport to have no interest in fame at all. Additionally, I shall attempt to incorporate my work as a media psychologist of long standing, having first appeared as a mental health broadcaster on radio in 1984, and on television in 1985. Additionally, I shall consider the aforementioned sexual fantasy data that I accumulated, principally between 2002 and 2007, as I now possess a unique database of the sexual fantasy preferences of approximately 25,000 British and American adults, including their preferred sexual fantasies about celebrities. Finally, I will incorporate some of my more direct knowledge as the husband of a professional singer, as well as my own experience of working in the public eye, having appeared in several television documentaries on psychological subjects and having worked as the Resident Psychotherapist for the British Broadcasting Corporation between 2004 and 2007.

Synthesising these various bodies of experience, I have arrived at the following hypotheses.

a. Celebrity worship and the family romance

I strongly concur with Sigmund Freud's aforementioned concept of the family romance as a key ingredient in the lust for fame and celebrity, based upon his clinical psychoanalytic experience and upon his direct observations of youngsters. As we have already noted, the universal childhood wish to adopt more exalted and more celebrated parents serves as a correction to a disappointing reality. As Freud (1909c, p. 239) noted, many children indulge "in a phantasy in which both his parents are replaced by others of better birth".[19]

Freud also commented, with great prescience, that a little boy or girl will, in certain cases, imagine not only having a new set of parents, but also a new childhood altogether, in which he or she has no more pesky siblings. As Freud (1909c, p. 240) explained, "An interesting variant of the family romance may then appear, in which the hero and author returns to legitimacy himself while his brothers and sisters are eliminated by being bastardized."[20] Perhaps this fleeting remark from 1909 can help us to understand more readily the current preoccupation with so-called "reality television" programmes such as *American Idol*, and *Big Brother*, and *I'm a Celebrity . . . Get Me Out of Here!*, in which viewers vote to "evict" a member of the television family each week, as though indulging in the symbolically transmogrified act of eliminating our sibling rivals one by one. If this notion contains any validity, it would certainly contribute to a better appreciation of the pervasive popularity of this highly rated genre of entertainment.

b.   Celebrity worship, object loss, and object use

Building upon Freud's studies in child psychology, Winnicott, as the veritable "cartographer of infancy" (Kahr, 2002a, p. 1), enriched the terrain quite considerably, fleshing out the map of our early years with exquisite detail. In terms of the psychology of celebrity lust, Winnicott (1935) has helped us to comprehend more fully our attraction to famous people based, in part, on our need to know the whereabouts of important figures in our lives, as a means of minimising object loss. Additionally, Winnicott (1969) wrote with frankness about our need to use objects, to control objects, and to allow ourselves as clinicians to become objects who might be used in exactly the same way in which fans use celebrities and, likewise, celebrities use fans. Winnicott's notion of object usage provides us with ample material for theorising about the nature of popular culture. One doubts, however, whether Donald Winnicott, who died long before the introduction of the personal computer or the internet, would have appreciated just *how* fully we have come to use celebrities.

Consider, for example, the B.B.C.'s on-line computer celebrity trading service, Celebdaq, which operated between 2002 and 2010 and which permitted participants to delight in watching the monetary value of a particular well-known personality rise and fall, like so much stock (Hensher, 2003). Moreover, we have the capability of using celebrities in far more sinister ways, and we shall examine in due course some examples of a more sadistic use of the famous.

Sigmund Freud abhorred the notion that lay people might slander great men. In his monograph on the psychology of the artist Leonardo da Vinci, Freud (1910a) quoted a fragment of verse from Friedrich Schiller's poem, "Das Mädchen von Orleans", which appeared as a prologue to Schiller's 1801 play, *Die Jungfrau von Orleans* [*The Maiden from Orleans*]:

> *Es liebt die Welt, das Strahlende zu schwärzen*
> *Und das Erhabene in den Staub zu ziehn.*
>
> [The world loves to black the radiant
> and drag the sublime into the dust.]

In this respect, Freud, too, could appreciate the ways in which we all use famous people as objects whom we can denigrate quite easily.

More recently, Dr Estela Welldon (2009, 2011), the noted forensic psychiatrist and pioneer of forensic psychotherapy and psychoanalysis, has elaborated upon the notions of Freud and Winnicott, commenting sagaciously about the way in which those who have achieved fame will often commit self-destructive acts that result in considerable shame (witness the actor Hugh Grant engaging in a sexual act with a prostitute). Whatever the sources of the celebrity's journey, which Welldon (2009, p. 162) has described as a trajectory "From fame to shame", we know that many people will indulge in object use and will derive conscious or unconscious pleasure from the humiliation of the celebrity as a means of enhancing their own fragile sense of esteem.

c.   **Celebrity worship and the primal scene: mother's face, voice, and scent**

In addition to the contributions of Sigmund Freud and Donald Winnicott, one must not omit Karl Menninger's (1937) simple but profound remark, based on his experience in Hollywood's Vendôme restaurant: namely, that we stare at movie stars in order to indulge our primal scene wish to see our mother's naked body, something that contemporary psychoanalytic workers would understand, perhaps more accurately, as a desire for primitive skin contact with our primary caregiving or attachment figure. Having practised psychiatry and psychoanalysis before the flourishing of the experimental developmental psychological research on facial recognition, Menninger would not have known the extent to which each of us, as infants, craves the sight of our mother's faces, and that we even possess the capacity, within hours after birth, to differentiate our own mother's face from that of other women of similar age and appearance (e.g., Bower, 1989). Similarly, we know from the important neonatological research of the paediatrician Dr Aidan Macfarlane (1975) that newborn infants can also discriminate the smell of the breast milk of their biological mothers from that of other lactating women who have recently given birth, and that babies can do so, once again, almost immediately. Similarly, infants can discern the sound of mother's voice, even while still *in utero* (e.g., deMause, 1981, 1982, 2002b).

65

Just as an adult might sit down with a D.V.D. or a book for entertainment, so the infant amuses himself or herself with an *Ur*-D.V.D.: namely, the sight, the smell, and the sound of the preoedipal mother of earliest infancy—the first celebrity worshipped by each of us. Our preoccupation with the mother's body parts manifests itself, symbolically, in our endless desire to see the faces of young celebrities in their late teens and early twenties, the age of most mothers at the time of birth. Advertising companies and film production companies appreciate this phenomenon quite intuitively, and thus, by parading posters of Betty Grable, Farah Fawcett, or Paris Hilton in front of us, through a process now known as "branding" or "marketing", they indulge our wish to see the face of one very special young woman with sparkling eyes, lustrous hair, and all the other characteristics of the young, idealised, primiparous mother.

By staring at the faces of our celebrities, by listening to their voices on iTunes, or on the radio, or in concert, and by sniffing their scent (through the purchase of the growing barrage of celebrity perfumes such as *Heat* by Beyoncé Knowles, *Fantasy* by Britney Spears, and *In Bloom* by Reese Witherspoon), we indulge an archaic wish to become reunited with the nurturant mother of infancy. Furthermore, we not only yearn to have renewed access to the face, voice, and scent of our mothers, but, additionally, we hope for *exclusive* access, hence our wish to penetrate the bedrooms of our celebrities by snooping into their private lives in the most relentless and, often, most invidious manner.

Building further upon these classical Freudian foundations, I have enumerated several interrelated theoretical strands and possibilities which will contribute to a more fully elaborated theory of fame-worship.

d. Celebrity as a defence against impotence and castration anxiety

In the Hollywood film *Bonnie and Clyde*, released in 1967, based upon the lives of the infamous American gangsters Bonnie Parker and Clyde Barrow, we discover that Barrow, portrayed by the film actor Warren Beatty, cannot make love to a woman, and thus he rebuffs the ardent advances of Parker, played by the actress Faye Dunaway. However, after Bonnie Parker writes a poem about Clyde Barrow, which she then arranges to have published in a newspaper, he exclaims in his Texan drawl, "You've made me somebody they gonna remember." And, thus, upon discovering himself to be *famous*—Barrow becomes aroused and then, at long last, engages in passionate love-making. One cannot, of course, confirm that the real Clyde Barrow, as opposed to the Hollywood version, actually struggled with impotence, but the film's director, Arthur Penn—a graduate of a long Freudian analysis with the German–American refugee clinician Dr Rudolph Loewenstein—suggested this as a psychologically plausible contribution to the script (Farber and Green, n.d.), one that might explain, perhaps, Barrow's need to carry an enormous phallic-shaped gun. Fame functions, in effect, as an aphrodisiac.

Indeed, becoming a celebrity serves as a temporary remedy for feeling ineffective and pusillanimous. Similarly, worshipping someone famous provides a sense of enhancement through identification with the presumed phallic potency of another. How many billions of flabby, out-of-shape, arthritic middle-aged and old men have jeopardised their marriages in order to devote long weekends watching young, vigorous, orthopaedically potent sporting heroes kick a ball across a stadium? Only through the process of fame-worship, or *identification with the celebrity*, can one experience an immediate sense of thrill, of power, of vitality, and of triumph over the fear of being castrated, either physically or psychologically.

e. Fame and celebrity as defences against loneliness and misattunement

Preoccupation with the fame of others provides an illusion of connection with those in the public eye. In this way, immersing oneself in the lives of others serves as a very powerful defence against solitariness. Indeed, countless numbers of television viewers have developed private worlds peopled by the cast of *EastEnders*, or *Coronation Street*, or *Desperate Housewives*, or, indeed, *The Archers*, at least in part as a means of combating such aloneness. Of course it would be naïve to deny that these television and radio programmes often provide genuinely engaging entertainment to many; yet part of the pleasure stems, however, *not* from the intellectual stimulation or comedy value inherent in these soap operas, but, rather, from the fact that these programmes furnish lonely people with a sense of community and a continuity of characters.

Years ago, I had the privilege of attending clinical supervision with Dr Susanna Isaacs Elmhirst, a child psychoanalyst who had inherited, upon Donald Winnicott's retirement, his post at the Paddington Green Children's Hospital in West London. I once presented a patient—a profoundly intellectually disabled person who spent the entire day watching soap operas—and I shall never forget Dr Elmhirst's wise observations. She asked me, "Do you know the real reason why people love soap operas?" I confessed that I did not, and I waited for Dr Elmhirst to enlighten me. She elaborated, "Because the *same* people keep coming back and back and *back* in episode after episode. They just keep coming back and back and *back*". Although soap operas and other dramas do kill off their characters from time to time, they do so sparingly for the most part, allowing viewers to develop cyber-relationships with the denizens of "Albert Square" in *EastEnders* or "The Rovers" in *Coronation Street* and thus mitigating the dreadful pain of object loss.

Having once worked with a compulsive autograph hunter who religiously collected the signatures of every famous actor or actress that she could find, I can confirm clinically that the wish to obtain these scribbled signatures served as both a creative and a desperate attempt to cling to some piece of the actor that could always keep the patient company. We track celebrities, we collect their autographs, we purchase their ruby-red slippers at auctions, and we even pretend to *become* them (witness the adolescent impersonating a pop star, replete with hairbrush and bedroom mirror); and we do so not only as a form of admiration and, perhaps, as a shrewd financial investment but, also, most fundamentally, as a means of correcting early experiences of loneliness, loss, and misattunement, and of not quite feeling famous enough ourselves in our families of origin. Staring at the celebrity may, in fact, represent a displacement of our own more primaeval wish to be seen.

In 2005, I had the opportunity to serve as the presenter, for a terrestrial broadcaster, of a television documentary, *Britain's Sexual Fantasies,* based upon my research project on the role of early child abuse and trauma in the genesis of sexual thoughts and constellations (Kahr, 2007a, 2008, 2015). During the making of the programme, we filmed a number of sequences outdoors. In the early morning of our first of day of production, I stood on the Millennium Bridge in South London, near the Globe Theatre, talking about the relationship between sexual fantasies and spousal infidelity. I had to spend absolutely ages on the bridge in the freezing cold, because, as members of the public passed by, quite a few jumped up behind me to wave at the cameras, and thus we had to re-shoot and re-shoot the scene, over and over again. Later in the afternoon, we undertook more filming on the streets of Covent Garden, as I talked about Freud's theories on fantasy. Once again, groups of young people kept interrupting the process, desperate to be seen by the camera, and thus necessitating further re-shooting of the sequence. Through this experience, I learned very powerfully about the incredibly strong need of people to be noticed (Kahr, 2006).

Clearly, many men and women felt excluded from the camera, and they wished, perhaps, to be enveloped by a large lens that might, symbolically, represent the adoring eyes of the mother. With such a working concept in mind, one could understand much more readily why so many young people felt the need to insinuate themselves into the camera shot.

f. Fame-worship as a defence against death and death anxiety

In 1980, the American film *Fame* burst onto cinema screens around the world. A finely wrought movie about the struggles of young performing-arts students desperate to find a niche for themselves in show business, this motion picture will perhaps be best remembered for Irene Cara's electric rendition of the title track, "Fame", written by Michael Gore and Dean Pitchford, a song that won an Academy Award. As Miss Cara and her comrades danced with abandon on top of New York City taxicabs, they exulted, "Fame! / I'm gonna live forever!" One need not be a psychologist to appreciate that the lust for fame incorporates the primitive wish to avoid death at all costs, and to live eternally.

Not only do we crave fame and its cousin, immortality, as a means of cheating the unbearable finitude of death, but we also delight in controlling death to the best of our ability. In the United States of America, certain office workers have, apparently, created a phenomenon that has come to be known as the "death pool" (Gritten, 2002, p. 54): using either aged celebrities or self-destructive celebrities as part of a game, they bet money on which famous person will die first, Katharine Hepburn versus Bob Hope (for example), or Robert Downey, Jr. versus Eminem. These office death pools or ghoul pools represent not only the expression of death wishes directed at famous, wealthy, talented celebrities, but they also serve as a primitive means of projecting all deathliness into someone else. By turning the anticipated death date of a celebrity into a betting matter, we burden celebrities with yet one further task: that of entertaining us not only in their lifetime but, also, in their incipient death. Perhaps the ghoul pool also allows us to attain some primitive control over the deeply unpredictable nature of human death, especially its timing.

g. Celebrities as targets of envy, destructiveness, and murderous rage

As we have already noted, Dr Donald Winnicott wrote creatively about the way in which each of us will use someone else, or a part of someone else, as an object, often for our very own primitive purposes. We might, perhaps, kick our cat, for example, as a means of discharging primitive destructive affects. In this way, the animal becomes a target for externalisation—an object for use. Similarly, we might scream at our psychotherapist, because we know that he or she will not, in all likelihood, retaliate and will also consent, perhaps therapeutically, perhaps masochistically, to tolerate this discharge, which no one else would.

One special case of object usage concerns the deeply primitive affect of human envy, a subject of special interest to psychotherapists and psychoanalysts, as envy becomes a source of deep pain and destructiveness in the human mind and within human relationships. Mrs Melanie Klein (1957, p. ix), the noted Austrian–British psychoanalyst and author of the foundational textbook on envy, described it as "a most potent factor in undermining feelings of love and gratitude at their root".

According to Klein, we express our enviousness in a multitude of attacks, sometimes of a verbal nature, sometimes of a physical nature. With reference to famous people, throughout the history of celebrity, one need not search very far for evidence of envy. For instance, virtually every famous individual has had to endure verbal assaults, often of a most envious and cruel, if not murderous, nature. In his *Naturalis Historiae*, Gaius Plinius Secundus, better known as the first-century Roman historian Pliny the Elder, took great delight in humiliating the empress Messalina, sometime wife of the emperor Claudius, as a mere prostitute, claiming that she had participated in an all-night sex orgy, servicing large numbers of customers. Some centuries later, Marie Antoinette, the deposed queen of France, had to endure similar public humiliation, including accusations, levied by the scandalmonger Jacques-René Hébert, of having engaged in a salacious, incestuous relationship with her young son, Louis Charles, the former *dauphin* of France (Haslip, 1987; Dunlop, 1993; Fraser, 2001).

And, in more recent times, the Tsaritsa Alexandra of Russia endured many envious assaults, lambasted for her ostensible sexual liaison with the monk Grigori Efimovich Rasputin (King, 1990; Cook, 2005).

Such calumniations invariably exert a very powerful effect. Having served as psychotherapist to many people in the public eye who have had to read vicious falsehoods about themselves in the press, I can confirm that such stories lacerate most deeply.

Envious attacks can not only be levied by means of verbal cruelty, they can even be unleashed in a far more concrete and physical form. When the American journalist Elsa Maxwell went to Hollywood in the spring of 1932, she spent her first night as a guest in the home of the popular film star Gary Cooper, who, in turn, had rented the house from the actress Greta Garbo. Miss Maxwell (1954, pp. 226–227) had great difficulty sleeping that evening because no sooner had she begun to unpack her clothing, she heard

> a sudden outbreak of frightful, bloodcurdling screaming and howling, as though all the demons in Southern California had their tails caught in the wringers. I looked out of the window and saw a sight that would have raised the hackles of a gargoyle. There were about twenty mature women in the driveway yowling like lovesick cats. Some were making horrible mewing noises and clawing frantically at the walls of the house.

Mr Cooper's housekeeper told Miss Maxwell that these women—all ardent fans—would come to the home every night, and that even the police could not keep them away.

In terms of attacks on celebrity walls, I remember that, during the 1990s, each week, on my way to a regular psychoanalytic meeting, I had to walk past the London residence of singer and recording artist Robbie Williams in Notting Hill. I became shocked at the sheer amount of graffiti, penned in thick black ink, scrawled by sexually rapacious fans with increasing intensity on the white walls of Mr Williams's maisonette. Eventually, he moved house.

These episodes represent only the *less* extreme forms of envious and sadistic attacks on the homes of celebrities. In the more sinister cases, our so-called "love" of celebrity becomes perverted into the forensic phenomenon of stalking or even murder—the ultimate manifestations of a deadly envy.

Celebrity-stalking occurs with great frequency in the upper echelons of show business; indeed, I have heard more than one famous person pontificate with pride that one can only *truly* regard oneself as famous when one can claim to have a deranged stalker in tow. Ursula Reichert-Habbishaw, the mother of four children, bombarded the film star Richard Gere with some one thousand e-mails, faxes, and telephone calls. Tragically, this actually represents the *less* extreme form of stalking. Envious stalking can become manifest in a much more vicious form (cf. Mullen, James, Meloy, Pathé, Farnham, Preston, Darnley, and Berman, 2009). In 1995, for example, the beautiful, 23-year-old Mexican–American singer Selena Quintanilla-Pérez, better known as "Selena", suffered a fatal gunshot wound to her back, fired by none other than Yolanda Saldívar, the president of the Texas branch of Selena's fan club. Certainly, fervent fandom can often serve as a thinly disguised defence against deathly wishes.

Murderous celebrity-stalking tends to blight the lives of the most famous and, hence, the most envied of public personalities. In 1932, Charles Augustus Lindbergh, the handsome, wealthy, and accomplished American aviator, known as "Lucky Lindy"—at that time one of the most famous men on the planet—suffered the unthinkable: namely, the kidnap and ultimate murder of his 20-month-old son,

Charles Augustus Lindbergh, Jr. As Leo Braudy (1986) has noted, the kidnapping and killing of Lindbergh's heir, an act known by many as the "Crime of the Century", remains one of the most chilling examples of an attack on a man who had flown, quite literally, higher than anyone else, having successfully piloted a monoplane by himself across the Atlantic Ocean in 1927. Hence, in the eyes of many, Lindbergh needed to be brought down to size. Horrifically, Lindbergh not only suffered from the pain of searching for his missing son, but he also had to endure solicitations from a boat builder from Virginia, one John Hughes Curtis, who claimed that he knew the location of the kidnapped baby, thus raising Lindbergh's hopes. Eventually, this crank confessed that he had led Lindbergh on a wild goose chase in the hope of becoming famous himself (Mosley, 1976). By that point, the child had already been murdered.

On 8 December 1980, at approximately 5.00 p.m., a 25-year-old Texas-born sometime security guard, one Mark David Chapman, caught sight of Beatle John Lennon outside the latter's lavish apartment building, The Dakota, on the Upper West Side of New York City. Chapman entreated Lennon to sign a copy of the British singer's recently released album, *Double Fantasy*. Some hours later, Chapman met Lennon again as he returned to his home and, at 10.49 p.m., fired five shots from a .38 calibre handgun, killing Lennon instantly (Norman, 2008). Afterwards, while in prison, Mark David Chapman confessed to the television journalist Barbara Walters, "I thought by killing him I would acquire his fame." This murder, in particular, reveals not only the horrors of envy towards the famous but, also, the painfully easy erosion between idealisation and denigration, between autograph-hunting fanship and the act of murder, which can never be undone.

h.   Celebrity and the urge to commit infanticide: the bedrock of the human mind

Thus far, I have identified some seven explanatory strands that might help us to comprehend the urge to engage in a relationship with celebrities: (1) a manifestation of the family romance, substituting our drab, ordinary parents with more spectacular, fantasmatic parents; (2) an expression of our need to control object loss and to engage in object use; (3) a concretisation of the primal scene and, consequently, a celebration of the face, voice, and scent of the preoedipal mother of infancy; (4) a defence against impotency and castration anxiety; (5) a defence against loneliness; (6) a defence against death and death anxiety; and (7) a form of envious attack, often of a murderous nature. According to my clinical experience, these seven strands will often overlap and, in so doing, will contribute to the potency of the wish to use and abuse our celebrities. In other words, we might scream and shout and rant when watching a pop star in an arena or a sports star in a stadium, not only because the celebrity entertains us but, also, because we have a multitude of often very unconscious reasons to engage in a connection with said celebrity.

In addition to the seven aforementioned contributory factors, I wish to highlight yet one more. This factor—the eighth—may have the greatest pull of them all: namely, the wish to commit the ritual infanticide of the youngest members of our civilisation.

But how on earth does infanticide relate to the question of fame and celebrity?

According to ancient Greek legend, the mythical king Minos of Crete, son of the god Zeus and the Phoenician-born mortal Europa, waged war against the Athenians and proved victorious. As part of his spoils, Minos demanded that, every nine years, the Athenians select seven of their most beautiful maidens and seven of their most handsome Athenian boys and then send them by ship to Crete, where, imprisoned in the king's diabolical labyrinth at Knossos, they would be devoured, sacrificially, by the infamous creature—half-bull, half-human—known as the Minotaur, who fed on flesh and blood. The ritual sacrifice of these youngsters continued unabated until one potential victim, young Theseus of Athens, a brave hero, vanquished the Minotaur. As the winner of the competition, Theseus became, accordingly, the founder-king of Athens.

This iconic tale of ancient sacrifice, of a bloody competition in which only one youthful participant arises victorious, has occupied an archetypal place in both Western and Eastern civilisation, and students of mythology will find elaborate versions of this very thematic in the stories of the Mesopotamian bull-man Shedu, in the tales of the Middle Eastern bull-man Moloch [Molech], in the legend of the Egyptian bull-man Apis, as well as in the exploits of the Japanese equivalent, Ushi-oni. Later representations of the Minotaur persist into the Middle Ages and the Renaissance, notably as the "*infamia di Creti*" in Dante Alighieri's *Inferno*, which constitutes the first part of *La Divina Commedia*, written in the early fourteenth century.

Myths do not originate out of thin air. They derive from long-standing, primitive experience. In this case, the sacrifice in mythology of the young can be traced to infanticidal child-rearing practices perpetrated by the ancient Africans, Celts, Chinese, Egyptians, Etruscans, Greeks, Hebrews, Hindus, Japanese, Magyars, Mesoamericans, Romans, and others, studied extensively by contemporary historians and psychohistorians, most notably by the American scholar Lloyd deMause (1974, 1990, 1991, 2002a), as well as by numerous other scholars (e.g., Kellum, 1974; Langer, 1974; Lyman, 1974; McLaughlin, 1974; Helmholz, 1975; Kahr, 1991, 1993, 1994a, 1994b, 1994c, 1996a, 1996b, 1997, 2001, 2002b, 2007c, 2007d, 2012; Miles, 2010) as well as by archaeologists (e.g., Stager and Wolff, 1984; Brown, 1991; cf. Miller, 2001). Psychoanalytic clinicians have also written widely about the ubiquitousness of parental death wishes towards babies, which will be enacted by more fragile parents, resulting in either the physical or the psychological destruction of the infant (e.g., Winnicott, 1949; Lidz, 1973; Bloch, 1978; Sinason, 2001).

Throughout history, our predecessors have compulsively repeated the Minotaurean destruction of young people, often in ritualised, repetitive ways. The ancient Carthaginians sacrificed their infants to the gods and placed them in vessels in the Tophet, an ancient burial ground containing numerous urns full of charred infant remains, which survives to this day (Stager and Wolff, 1984; Brown, 1991). Often infants would be sacrificed, but sometimes those slain would be teenagers rather than babies. The ancient Moche of Northern Peru, a Pre-Colombian people who flourished in the first millennium of the Common Era, sacrificed newly pubescent youngsters; and a contemporary archaeologist–anthropologist, Professor Steve Bourget (2006) of the University of Texas at Austin, has uncovered the osteological remains of these ritual killings (cf. Bourget and Jones, 2008; Hocquenghem, 2008; Uceda, 2008; Verano, 2008; Gaither, Kent, Bethard, Vasquez, and Rosales, 2016; Klaus and Shimada, 2016), thus offering further proof of the human need to kill our offspring.

Minotaur-style executions, in group formation, have occurred in virtually every epoch of human history and in every culture, ranging from the gladiatorial combats of ancient Rome, to the Colonial witch trials in Salem, Massachusetts, to the guillotines of late-eighteenth-century France, to contemporary warfare, which involves the transportation of young men and women in the military, often on ships, to meet their death overseas. Centuries ago, these tribal group murders would have taken the form of actual slaughter, as with the ancient child sacrifices. Sometimes the executions would be staged more symbolically. In 513 B.C.E. Cleisthenes, an Attic Greek aristocrat from Athens who claimed descent from Herakles, introduced a new form of public execution, the *ostrakon*, from which the word "ostracism" derives. The *ostrakon* refers literally to a piece of broken pottery, and Cleisthenes, one of the founders of modern democracy, devised a system whereby Athenians would inscribe the name of the individual they most wished to evict from the city on the *ostrakon* pottery, usually a person of fame and fortune. This may well be the first historical instance of calling an 0800 number to evict one's most despised celebrity.

Ancient infanticide, Minotaurean sacrifices of the teenagers, and Athenian *ostrakon* voting persist to this day in symbolic form. They persist in our current crop of reality television programmes, such as *The X Factor* and *American Idol* and others too numerous to mention, as well as in films such as *The Hunger Games*, in which youngsters would be sacrificed, one by one, until a winner can be chosen.[21] Often, these thinly disguised public executions will be facilitated by youthful women, such as Cheryl Cole or Dannii Minogue or Nicole Scherzinger, who represent the young infanticidal, preoedipal mothers of infancy who orchestrate the sacrifice of the modern equivalent of the beautiful Athenian virgins.

In certain programmes, such the B.B.C.'s *Over the Rainbow*, celebrity judges would evict potential West End starlets each week, but viewers at home would have the right to "save" their favourite participant. This increasingly widely spread format-point, that of "saving" a victim from execution, serves as a defence mechanism against the more invidious assassination and thus helps viewers to feel less guilty about their enjoyment of the Minotaurean sacrifice in which they have participated.

The Roman author Lucius Mestrius Plutarchus, better known as Plutarch, and the Christian Berber writer Quintus Septimius Florens Tertullianus, better remembered as Tertullian, had reminded us that, often, children slated for sacrifice would be required to offer their consent beforehand. Perhaps the long queues of young girls who had hoped to play the role of "Dorothy Gale" in Baron Lloyd Webber's stage production of *The Wizard of Oz* serve as the modern reincarnation of the ancient children who had to authorise their own assassination. In terms of the notion of object use, perhaps human beings harbour a profound need to create celebrities and then worship them, albeit temporarily, so that we can then murder them off, as our ancestors did, in a highly symbolic ritual, masked by beautiful music and costumes—thus hiding the evil of the executions that await them in the wings.

SIX

"I'm a celebrity and I don't even know it": on becoming famous in one's own household

I am: yet what I am none cares or knows,
My friends forsake me like a memory lost.

John Clare, "I Am", circa 1844–1845

At the age of 24 years, the aspiring stage and film actor Frank Langella (2012, p. 354) asked the multimillionairess Rachel "Bunny" Mellon, "What should I do when I meet a famous person?" Mrs Mellon replied, "Don't think too much about famous people. They already think too much about themselves" (quoted in Langella, 2012, p. 354).

In this short essay, I have endeavoured to think, *not* about the celebrities themselves, but, rather, about those who venerate the celebrities. One could, perhaps, regard this as an effort to understand something more about the psychology of the crowd.

The world of celebrity and fame might be described as one of great toxicity. In his famous song "Don't Put Your Daughter on the Stage, Mrs Worthington", published in 1935, Noël Coward advised aspiring theatrical mothers everywhere not to encourage their children to pursue a career in show business. As a lifelong participant in the world of fame and celebrity, Coward knew of its dangers only too well. Some writers have suggested that fame produces breakdown (e.g., Wallace, 1986). Others have hypothesised that those entranced by celebrity all suffer from histrionic personality disorder (Gritten, 2002). The American film star Tyrone Power referred to his stalking fans as "the monster" (quoted in Gritten, 2002, p. 45). Another American movie actor, Tony Curtis, compared fame to Alzheimer's Disease, noting, "You don't know anybody, but they all know you" (quoted in Gritten, 2002, p. 45). At least one researcher had discovered that celebrities not only suffer from a higher likelihood of cirrhosis of the liver, kidney disease, and ulcers and live shorter lives, but, additionally, will be more likely to commit suicide or to be murdered than the average citizen (Fowles, 1992).

Some time after she had taken the theatrical world by storm as the original "Cassie" in the internationally acclaimed 1975 Broadway musical *A Chorus Line*, the Tony-Award-winning actress and dancer Donna McKechnie found herself unemployed, reclusive, depressive, and feeling quite sorry for herself, while at home hoovering. Ms McKechnie then began to watch a popular American quiz programme called *Jeopardy*. As she recalled, "I'm watching *Jeopardy* on television and *I'm one of the answers!* In this game show! And I'm going, 'Boo hoo, boo hoo, I'm a celebrity and I don't even know it!'" (quoted in Flinn, 1989, p. 113). Years later, Ms McKechnie (personal communication, 24 October 2009) summed up her years in show business thus: "Glamour is my life and the rats are running through the dressing room." In many respects, these anecdotes encapsulate some of the arguably perverse ingredients of being a famous, award-winning star, waiting desperately for one's unemployment cheque to arrive in the post.

Perhaps Dante Alighieri encapsulated fame best in his admonition, inscribed in the *Purgatorio*, the second part of *La Divina Commedia*: "*Non è il mondan romore altro ch'un fiato / di vento, ch'or vien quinci e or vien quindi*" ["Your earthly fame is but a gust of wind / that blows about, shifting this way and that"]. Or perhaps we might remember the wariness of Emily Dickinson, who, in a brief poem written circa 1861, exclaimed:

> How dreary—to be—Somebody!
> How public—like a Frog—
> To tell your name—the livelong June—
> To an admiring Bog!

And yet, in spite of its horrors, celebrity culture continues to exert the most primitive of influence upon the famous, upon those who crave fame, and upon those who fan the flames of fame. Celebrity and its worship will not disappear, even when subjected to sustained psychoanalytic scrutiny.

We know that the world of fame contains many malignant components, and we need not reiterate these here. But we must wonder whether we might we be able to identify any positive aspects of celebrity worship. Although I have not focused on these as comprehensively as I have concentrated upon the negative features, I have come to the conclusion that celebrity culture has immense benefits for fans. Celebrities entertain us, they help us to laugh, they facilitate play, and they provide us with non-prescription antidepressant medication. As "Lina Lamont", the intellectually-challenged screen goddess, brilliantly portrayed by Jean Hagen in the 1952 musical film *Singin' in the Rain*, chirped to her fans: "If we bring a little joy into your humdrum lives, it makes us feel as though our hard work ain't been in vain for nothing. Bless you all."

Furthermore, celebrities function as aspirational role models to young people and, perhaps, to the not so young as well. They provide us with stories of success, of conquest over adversity, of survival from cancer and other painful diseases. They also offer us a sense of community and create so-called water-cooler moments—"shared national experiences" (Hattersley, 2009, p. 18) that allow us to feel part of a community, especially when, the next day in the office, we compare notes on the previous evening's news items and offer our reviews of popular, much-watched television programmes.

Old-timers might balk that fame should be accorded only to the Marie Curies, the Albert Einsteins, and the Nelson Mandelas of the world, mindful of the ancient Latin epithet "famam extendere factis" ["to spread abroad his fame by deeds"]. The Victorians embraced this philosophy of fame, and those of us who live or work in North London can easily drive past the William Ellis School in Highgate (established in 1862 as the Gospel Oak Schools) and derive inspiration from the institution's motto, chiselled on its outer wall: "Rather Use Than Fame." Clearly, the notion of fame will always have its proponents and its critics, and each of us will pursue a different model of fame, some craving international acclaim, some desirous of recognition by colleagues within a peer community, others requiring only the appreciation of their spouses, parents, children, and friends.

Whatever our final view about celebrity and its healthfulness or, indeed, its malignancies, modern fame—early twenty-first-century fame—has adopted new contours. Dr Brendan MacCarthy (personal communication, 26 March 2003), the distinguished British psychoanalyst and child psychiatrist, told me that when he began to practise in the 1950s and 1960s, he did not remember any youngsters expressing a wish to become famous. Little boys, for instance, hoped that they might, perhaps, train as astronauts, or be rich, but they did not fantasise about careers in film and television. Contemporary youngsters, however, have a different experience, and for many fame has become a career choice that threatens to sit alongside medicine, the law, psychotherapy, academia, accountancy, and graphic design. Should this phenomenon of fame as a *profession* cause alarm, or, indeed, admiration?

Some would maintain, of course, that fame must never be a goal, merely an unexpected outcome of having achieved great works. Others would argue that the endless stream of minimally educated men and women and children from economically straitened backgrounds who appear on our television screens in search of two minutes of fame on *Britain's Got Talent* might represent not a *deterioration* of civilisation as we know it, but, rather, its *democratisation*—a watershed era in human history akin to the emergence, from the margins and the shadows of our culture, of women, of the disabled, of ethnic groups and sexual minorities. For years, we prevented anyone who could not speak the King's English or, more recently, the Queen's English, from broadcasting on our radio sets or from appearing on our television screens. But through the democratisation of fame, everyone now has permission to join the party.

Although we might lambaste those in search of fame as hysterical and narcissistic and diagnose the modern media, likewise, as corrupt and perverse, perhaps the fame-seekers, the fame-producers, and the fame-supporters serve, above all, as a reminder that each of us craves a platform and *deserves* one. As Bishop George Berkeley, the eighteenth-century Irish philosopher, sloganised, "*Esse est percipi*" ["To be is to be perceived"]. Perhaps it may not be accidental that just as the popularity of reality television programmes continues to swell, so, too, does the demand for psychotherapy. Once having considered psychotherapy an American-style indulgence or a last resort for seemingly "crazy" people, today Britons everywhere have begun to embrace with increasing seriousness and sympathy the potentialities and benefits of psychotherapy and psychoanalysis. It may be that British men and women have finally come to recognise that psychotherapy offers a profound opportunity for clients or patients to feel famous and celebrated. After all, the psychotherapist provides a spotlight for each client, placing him or her centre stage for fifty minutes, with no competition from pesky understudies or cut-throat members of the chorus. Psychotherapy allows those in search of greater peace of mind and richer meaning in their lives an opportunity to star in their own autobiography instead of remaining on the sidelines of their lives, as so many millions of people seem to do.

Before we conclude this disquisition on celebrity and fame, let us recall not only our wish but, also, our *need* and *necessity* to be perceived, whether on screen, in the lecture theatre, in the consulting room or, more pressingly, at the family supper table. In order to achieve mental health, we must tolerate *not* being seen; we must accept and, indeed, enjoy anonymity, rather than insist upon being the narcissistic centre of attention. And yet, at the same time, we must also be seen and enjoy being seen. As the twentieth-century man of letters, Lytton Strachey (1918, p. 168), sagely observed, our lives often consist of "the mingled satisfactions of obscurity and fame". Each of us needs to grapple with obscurity, and each of us, likewise, needs some sort of fame, whether on screen or in the bosom of our homes. Perhaps we may come to recognise that the craze for international celebrity speaks symptomatically to the failure of so many parents and partners and children to celebrate their nearest and dearest at home.

In examining fame and celebrity, Sigmund Freud remains a beacon of inspiration, owing to his recognition that the urge to live an exalted, regal, famous life stems predominantly from infantile disappointment. If only mothers and fathers of the future could apply themselves even more fully to the recognition of their babies and thus make them feel like stars, one suspects that the urge to appear on *Pop Idol* or on *The X Factor* would become far less pressing.

NOTES

1. The original German passage reads: "der ersten schwärmerischen Leidenschaft eines Jünglings für eine gefeierte Künsterlin, die er hoch über sich stehend glaubt, und zu der er seinen Blick nur schüchtern zu erheben wagt" (Freud, 1920a, p. 13).
2. The original German passage reads: "Es ist gewöhnlich, daß Mutter, denen das Schicksal ein krankes oder sonst benachteiligtes Kind geschenkt hat, es für diese ungerechte Zurücksetzung durch ein Übermaß von Liebe zu entschädigen suchen. In dem zur Rede stehenden Falle benahm sich die stolze Mutter anders, sie entzog dem Kind ihre Liebe wegen seines Gebrechens. Als aus dem Kinde ein großmächtiger Mann geworden war, bewies dieser durch seine Handlungen unzweideutig, daß er der Mutter nie verziehen hatte" (Freud, 1933a, p. 93).
3. The original German sentence reads: "Ach, an Ruhm haben sie mich alle überflügelt, aber nicht an Glück und nicht an Zufriedenheit, wenn Du mein wirst" (Freud, 1884a, p. 126).
4. The original German passage reads: "Die Erwartung des ewigen Nachruhms war so schön" (Freud, 1897a, p. 285).
5. The original German passage reads: "Die Teilnahme der Bevölkerung ist sehr groß. Es regnet auch jetzt schon Glückwünsche und Blumenspenden, als sei die Rolle der Sexualität plötzlich von Sr. Majestät amtlich anerkannt, die Bedeutung des Traumes vom Ministerrat bestätigt und die Notwendigkeit einer psychoanalytischen Therapie der Hysterie mit 2/3 Majorität im Parlament durchgedrungen" (Freud, 1902a, p. 503).
6. Sigmund Freud's (1904) book on everyday psychopathology had appeared in a second edition in 1907 (Freud, 1907), so we cannot know which version the cabin boy may have read—very possibly the latter.

7. When the beautiful and glamorous American debutante Miss Brenda Diana Duff Frazier, a member of the 1930s "Café Society", became a teenage celebrity, she received innumerable fan letters from all over the world. Due to her tremendous fame, admirers did not require her postal address in order to write to her. One man from Nashville, Tennessee, addressed an envelope thus: "Brenda Frazier / New York, N.Y." (Diliberto, 1987, p. 117) and affixed a photograph of the debutante as well. The letter certainly reached its recipient, and it remained preserved in one of Miss Frazier's many scrapbooks.

8. The original German passage reads: "Die Analyse ist Pornographie; die Analytiker gehören also in den Kerker" (Ferenczi, 1911a, p. 354).

9. The original German passage reads: "Die negative Seite meines Ruhmes ist freilich noch stärker; gelegentlich ärgere ich mich, daß niemand auf Sie schimpft" (Freud, 1910b, p. 417).

10. The spelling of this fictitious name varies, depending upon the source. Robert Kimball (1971, p. 107), the eminent Cole Porter scholar, has used, variously, "Mr. and Mrs. S. Beach Fitch", as well as "Mr. and Mrs. S. Beech Fitch" (Kimball, 1983, p. 109), while Ethan Mordden (2010, p. 200), historian of the American musical theatre, has opted solely for "Mr. and Mrs. S. Beech Fitch".

11. In the interests of historical accuracy, I have chosen to refer to Geoffrey Chaucer's text as "Hous of Fame", rather than as "House of Fame", the title by which it has become more commonly known to contemporary audiences.

12. Naturally, this phrase deploys the sixteenth-century spelling of "haue" rather than "have", as well as the device of "permanēt", with a straight line over the second use of the letter "e", rather than "permanent".

13. It may be that William Blount, Lord Mountjoy, wrote this letter by himself. But it might well be that Mountjoy's scribe, Andreas Amonius, produced the letter to Desiderius Erasmus on his master's behalf.

14. In modern English, this phrase would read: "the just reward for their virtue".

15. The original German phrase reads: "der Erfüllung von Wünschen" (Freud, 1909a, p. 65).

16. The original German phrase reads: "der Korrektur des Lebens" (Freud, 1909a, p. 65).

17. The original German passage reads: "die Phantasie des Kindes mit der Aufgabe, die jetzt gering geschätzten Eltern loszuwerden und durch in der Regel sozial höher stehende zu ersetzen" (Freud, 1909a, p. 65).

18. The original German reads: "Familienromane" (Freud, 1909a, p. 65).

19. The original German passage reads: "in einer Phantasie findet, welche beide Eltern durch vornehmere ersetzt" (Freud, 1909a, p. 66).

20. The original German passage reads: "Eine interessante Variante dieses Familienromans ist es dann, wenn der dichtende Held für sich selbst zur Legitimät zurückkehrt, während er die anderen Geschwister auf diese Art also illegitim beseitigt" (Freud, 1909a, p. 67).

21. During the 1970s, Hollywood created an altogether cunning version of the sacrifice of the Athenian youngsters in a series of so-called "disaster" movies, such as *The Poseidon Adventure*, *Earthquake*, and *The Towering Inferno*, in which audience members became attached to the major characters, many of whom gradually died off, one by one, until only a small handful survived. Such motion pictures—all hugely popular at the time—provided viewers with an opportunity to experience death at close quarters, indulging the infantile wish to cheat mortality, which each cinema-goer would have done after exiting the deadly motion picture theatre safely. The cinematic genre of the disaster movie evoked not only the ancient infanticidal rituals of yore but, also, what Sigmund Freud (1917) described so compellingly as the wish to eliminate our sibling rivals.

ACKNOWLEDGEMENTS

I presented an abbreviated version of this book as the Lionel Monteith Memorial Lecture, sponsored by the Lincoln Clinic and Centre for Psychotherapy, London, held in the Governors' Hall at St. Thomas' Hospital in London, on 24 April 2010. I thank Ms Serena Heller and her committee for their kind invitation and, also, Mrs Aishleen Lester for having administered the lecture so efficiently. I also wish to extend my gratitude to Professor Jeremy Holmes for offering a helpful anecdote, and to Dr Valerie Sinason for her sagacious observations. Furthermore, I owe a great debt to my colleagues, Professor Caroline Bainbridge and Professor Candida Yates, the founders of "Media and the Inner World", a remarkable research network devoted to the application of psychoanalytic ideas to cultural matters; and I offer further appreciation to fellow psychocultural experts Dr Laura Bunt-MacRury, Professor Iain MacRury, and Professor Barry Richards. I would also like to convey my thanks to the following individuals for useful comments and contributions: Mrs Elissa Abrahams, Mr Marcel Berlins, Mr Dan Chambers, Ms Lisa Forrell, Dr Earl Hopper, Ms Jane Wynn Owen, Dr Amita Sehgal, Dr Estela

Welldon, Mr Paul Wilmshurst, and Mr John Woodhall. I wish to convey my warmest affection to Mr Oliver Rathbone, Publisher and Managing Director of Karnac Books, for having commissioned this volume, as well as his colleagues Ms Cecily Blench, Ms Constance Govindin, Ms Kate Pearce, and Dr Rod Tweedy for their assistance. After the sale of Karnac Books to Routledge / Taylor and Francis Group, Mr Russell George and his assistant Dr Elliott Morsia took charge of the typescript with tremendous conviviality and reliability. I have greatly enjoyed working with these two skilled and gracious men. I also wish to convey my thanks to Ms Naomi Hill of Routledge for having shepherded the book through production. And I owe the deepest of thanks, as ever, to the remarkable Mr Eric King and Mrs Klara Majthényi King at Communication Crafts – the best copy-editors of all – with whom I have had the privilege of working on many previous books.

REFERENCES

Advertising and Audiences: State of the Media. May 2014 (2014). New York: Nielsen Company. [http://www.nielsen.com/content/dam/nielsenglobal/jp/docs/report/2014/Nielsen_Advertising_and_%20Audiences%20Report-FINAL.pdf; Accessed on 12 March 2017].

Allen, Steve (2015). *So You Want to Be a Celebrity?* London: Elliott & Thompson.

Anonymous (2011). 2011: In Quotes. *The New Review. The Observer*, 18 December, p. 10.

Anonymous (n.d.). Untitled Newspaper Cutting. n.d. In Robert Kimball (Ed.), *Cole*, p. 108. New York: Holt, Rinehart and Winston, 1971.

Baily, Lionel (1973). *Gilbert and Sullivan and Their World*. London: Thames & Hudson.

Bainbridge, Caroline (2014). "Cinematic Screaming" or "All About My Mother": Lars von Trier's Cinematic Extremism as Therapeutic Encounter. In Caroline Bainbridge and Candida Yates (Eds.), *Media and the Inner World: Psycho-Cultural Approaches to Emotion, Media and Popular Culture*, pp. 53–68. Houndmills, Basingstoke, Hampshire: Palgrave Macmillan/Macmillan Publishers.

Bainbridge, Caroline, and Yates, Candida (2007). Everything to Play for: Masculinity, Trauma and the Pleasures of DVD Technologies. In Caroline Bainbridge, Susannah Radstone, Michael Rustin, and Candida Yates (Eds.), *Culture and the Unconscious*, pp. 107–122. Houndmills, Basingstoke, Hampshire: Palgrave Macmillan/Palgrave Macmillan Division of St. Martin's Press.

Balzac, Honoré de (n.d. [1920]). *La Peau de chagrin: Roman philosophique.* Vienna: Manz, Éditeur.

Barbas, Samantha (2001). *Movie Crazy: Fans, Stars, and the Cult of Celebrity.* New York: Palgrave.

Beresford, Philip (2010). *The Sunday Times Rich List 2010. The Sunday Times*, 25 April, pp. 4–5, 7–10, 12, 14–26, 28–39, 41–75, 78–83, 85–96, 98–102.

Berg, Alban (1923). Letter to Helene Berg, 29 November. In *Briefe an seine Frau*, pp. 532–533. München: Albert Langen/Georg Müller, Georg Müller Verlag, 1965.

Bertin, Célia (1982). *La Dernière Bonaparte.* Paris: Librairie Académique Perrin.

Bijaoui, Rémy (1996). *Prisonniers et prisons de la Terreur.* Paris: Auzas Éditeurs Imago/Éditions Imago.

Bion, Wilfred R. (1961). *Experiences in Groups and Other Papers.* London: Tavistock Publications.

Bloch, Dorothy (1978). *"So the Witch Won't Eat Me": Fantasy and the Child's Fear of Infanticide.* Boston, MA: Houghton Mifflin Company.

Blount, William [Lord Mountjoy] (1509). Letter to Desiderius Erasmus. 27 May. In Desiderius Erasmus, *Opus Epistolarvm Des. Erasmi Roterdami: Tom. I. 1484–1514*, Percy S. Allen (Ed.), pp. 449–452. Oxford: Typographeo Clarendoniano, 1906.

Boitani, Piero (1984). *Chaucer and the Imaginary World of Fame.* Cambridge: D.S. Brewer; Totowa, NJ: Barnes & Noble; Woodbridge, Suffolk: Boydell & Brewer.

Botham, Noel (2002). *Valentino: The First Superstar.* London: Metro/Metro Publishing.

Bourget, Steve (2006). *Sex, Death, and Sacrifice in Moche Religion and Visual Culture*. Austin, TX: University of Texas Press.

Bourget, Steve, and Jones, Kimberly L. (2008). Introduction. In Steve Bourget and Kimberly L. Jones (Eds.), *The Art and Archaeology of the Moche: An Ancient Andean Society of the Peruvian North Coast*, pp. ix–xiii. Austin, TX: University of Texas Press.

Bower, Thomas G. R. (1989). *The Rational Infant: Learning in Infancy*. New York: W.H. Freeman and Company.

Braudy, Leo (1986). *The Frenzy of Renown: Fame and its History*. New York: Oxford University Press.

Brown, Shelby (1991). *Late Carthaginian Child Sacrifice and Sacrificial Monuments in Their Mediterranean Context*. Sheffield: JSOT Press/Sheffield Academic Press.

Castle, Charles, and Tauber, Diana Napier (1971). *This Was Richard Tauber*. London: W.H. Allen/W.H. Allen and Company.

Chapman, James (2003). Do You Suffer from Celebrity Worship Syndrome? *Daily Mail*, 14 April, p. 25.

Chaucer, Geoffrey (c. 1379–1380). The House of Fame. In *The Poetical Works of Geoffrey Chaucer: Vol. V*, Richard Morris (Ed.), pp. 209–275. Covent Garden, London: George Bell and Sons, 1888.

Chernow, Ron (1993). *The Warburgs: A Family Saga*. New York: Random House.

Chierichetti, David (1976). *Hollywood Costume Design*. New York: Harmony Books.

Cook, Andrew (2005). *To Kill Rasputin: The Life and Death of Grigori Rasputin*. Brimscombe Port, Stroud, Gloucestershire: Tempus/Tempus Publishing.

Coward, Noël (1955a). Sunday 31 July. In *The Noel Coward Diaries*, Graham Payn and Sheridan Morley (Eds.), p. 277. London: George Weidenfeld & Nicolson, 1982.

Coward, Noël (1955b). Sunday 7 August. In *The Noel Coward Diaries*, Graham Payn and Sheridan Morley (Eds.), pp. 278–279. London: George Weidenfeld & Nicolson, 1982.

Coward, Noël (1958). Sunday 17 August. In *The Noel Coward Diaries*, Graham Payn and Sheridan Morley (Eds.), pp. 383–384. London: George Weidenfeld & Nicolson, 1982.

Coward, Noël (1965a). Wednesday 23 June. In *The Noel Coward Diaries*, Graham Payn and Sheridan Morley (Eds.), pp. 601–602. London: George Weidenfeld & Nicolson, 1982.

Coward, Noël (1965b). Sunday 4 July. In *The Noel Coward Diaries*, Graham Payn and Sheridan Morley (Eds.), pp. 602–603. London: George Weidenfeld & Nicolson, 1982.

Davies, Hunter (1968). *The Beatles: The Authorised Biography*. London: Heinemann/William Heinemann.

Day, Elizabeth (2017). Being Human: After Becoming Every Teen's Pin-Up and (Reluctantly) One of the Most Recognisable Faces in Hollywood, Robert Pattinson is Keen to Put the Twilight Years Behind Him. *Telegraph Magazine*, 4 November, pp. 14–15, 17, 19.

Delany, Sheila (1972). *Chaucer's House of Fame: The Poetics of Skeptical Fideism*. Chicago, IL: University of Chicago Press.

deMause, Lloyd (1974). The Evolution of Childhood. In Lloyd deMause (Ed.), *The History of Childhood*, pp. 1–73. New York: Psychohistory Press, Division of Atcom.

deMause, Lloyd (1981). The Fetal Origins of History. *Journal of Psychohistory*, *9*, 1–89.

deMause, Lloyd (1982). *Foundations of Psychohistory*. New York: Creative Roots.

deMause, Lloyd (1990). The History of Child Assault. *Journal of Psychohistory*, *18*, 1–29.

deMause, Lloyd (1991). The University of Incest. *Journal of Psychohistory*, *19*, 123–164.

deMause, Lloyd (2002a). *The Emotional Life of Nations*. New York: Karnac Books/Other Press.

deMause, Lloyd (2002b). The Personality of the Foetus. In Brett Kahr (Ed.), *The Legacy of Winnicott: Essays on Infant and Child Mental Health*, pp. 39–49. London: Karnac Books/Other Press.

Diderot, Denis (1765–1767). Correspondance avec Falconet. In *Mémoires, correspondance et ouvrages inédits de Diderot, publiés d'après les manuscrits confiés, en mourant, par l'auteur à Grimm: Tome troisième*, pp. 197–459. Paris: Paulin, Libraire-Éditeur/Alexandre Mesnier, Libraire, 1831.

Diderot, Denis (1766). Letter to Étienne Maurice Falconet. n.d. February. In Denis Diderot (1765–1767), Correspondance avec Falconet, pp. 210–268. In *Mémoires, correspondance et ouvrages inédits de Diderot, publiés d'après les manuscrits confiés, en mourant, par l'auteur à Grimm: Tome troisième*, pp. 197–459. Paris: Paulin, Libraire-Éditeur/ Alexandre Mesnier, Libraire, 1831.

Diliberto, Gioia (1987). *Debutante: The Story of Brenda Frazier*. New York: Alfred A. Knopf.

Dunlop, Ian (1993). *Marie-Antoinette: A Portrait*. London: Sinclair-Stevenson/Reed Consumer Books.

Eissler, Kurt R. (n.d.). Unpublished Note, 29 July. Box 122. Folder 13. Sigmund Freud Papers. Sigmund Freud Collection. Manuscript Reading Room, Room 101, Manuscript Division, James Madison Memorial Building, Library of Congress, Washington, D.C., U.S.A.

Ellenberger, Henri-F. (1977). L'Histoire d'"Emmy von N". *Evolution Psychiatrique*, *42*, 519–540.

Ellmann, Richard (1987). *Oscar Wilde*. London: Hamish Hamilton/ Penguin Books.

Elyot, Thomas (1531). *The Boke Named The Gouernour: In Two Volumes. Vol. II*, Henry Herbert Stephen Croft (Ed.). London: C. Kegan Paul and Company, 1880.

Embden, Heinrich Georg (1910). Ärztlicher Verein zu Hamburg: Sitzung vom 29 März 1910. *Neurologisches Centralblatt*, *29*, 659–662.

Farber, Stephen, and Green, Marc (1993). *Hollywood on the Couch: A Candid Look at the Overheated Love Affair between Psychiatrists and Moviemakers*. New York: William Morrow and Company.

Farber, Stephen, and Green, Marc (n.d.). Interview with Arthur Penn. n.d. Cited in Stephen Farber and Marc Green, *Hollywood on the*

Couch: A Candid Look at the Overheated Love Affair between Psychiatrists and Moviemakers. New York: William Morrow and Company, 1993.

Feldman, Sandor S. (1975). Discussion. *Psychoanalytic Forum,* 5, pp. 99–100. New York: International Universities Press.

Ferenczi, Sándor (1911a). Letter to Sigmund Freud, 16 February. In Sigmund Freud and Sándor Ferenczi, *Briefwechsel: Band I/1. 1908–1911*, Eva Brabant, Ernst Falzeder, Patrizia Giampieri-Deutsch, and André Haynal (Eds.), pp. 354–355. Vienna: Böhlau Verlag/Böhlau Verlag Gesellschaft, 1993.

Ferenczi, Sándor (1911b). Letter to Sigmund Freud, 16 February. In Sigmund Freud and Sándor Ferenczi, *The Correspondence of Sigmund Freud and Sándor Ferenczi: Volume 1, 1908–1914*, Eva Brabant, Ernst Falzeder, Patrizia Giampieri-Deutsch, and André Haynal (Eds.), Peter T. Hoffer (Transl.), pp. 255–256. Cambridge, MA: Belknap Press of Harvard University Press, 1993.

Flinn, Denny Martin (1989). *What They Did for Love: The Untold Story Behind the Making of* A Chorus Line. New York: Bantam Books.

Fowles, Jib (1992). *Starstruck: Celebrity Performers and the American Public.* Washington, D.C.: Smithsonian Institution Press.

Fraser, Antonia (2001). *Marie Antoinette: The Journey.* London: Weidenfeld & Nicolson/Orion Publishing Group.

Freud, Harry (n.d.). My Uncle. Unpublished Typescript. Box 9. Harry Freud Papers. Sigmund Freud Collection. Manuscript Reading Room, Room 101, Manuscript Division, James Madison Memorial Building, Library of Congress, Washington, D.C., U.S.A.

Freud, Martha (1938). Letter to Adolfine Freud, Marie Freud, Rosa Graf, and Pauline Winternitz, 22 June. Cited in Ronald W. Clark, *Freud: The Man and the Cause.* New York: Random House, 1980.

Freud, Sigmund (1884a). Letter to Martha Bernays, 17 November. In Sigmund Freud, *Briefe: 1873–1939*, Ernst L. Freud (Ed.), pp. 125–126. Frankfurt am Main: S. Fischer Verlag, 1960.

Freud, Sigmund (1884b). Letter to Martha Bernays, 17 November. In Sigmund Freud, *Letters of Sigmund Freud*, Ernst L. Freud (Ed.), Tania Stern and James Stern (Transls.), pp. 126–127. New York: Basic Books, 1960.

Freud, Sigmund (1897a). Letter to Wilhelm Fliess, 21 September. In Sigmund Freud. *Briefe an Wilhelm Fliess 1887–1904: Ungekürzte Ausgabe*, Jeffrey Moussaieff Masson and Michael Schröter (Eds.), pp. 283–286. Frankfurt am Main: S. Fischer/S. Fischer Verlag, 1986.

Freud, Sigmund (1897b). Letter to Wilhelm Fliess, 21 September. In Sigmund Freud. *The Complete Letters of Sigmund Freud to Wilhelm Fliess: 1887–1904*, Jeffrey Moussaieff Masson (Ed.), Lottie Newman, Marianne Loring, and Jeffrey Moussaieff Masson (Transls.), pp. 264–266. Cambridge, MA: Belknap Press of Harvard University Press, 1985.

Freud, Sigmund (1902a). Letter to Wilhelm Fliess, 11 March. In Sigmund Freud, *Briefe an Wilhelm Fliess 1887–1904: Ungekürzte Ausgabe*, Jeffrey Moussaieff Masson and Michael Schröter (Eds.), pp. 501–503. Frankfurt am Main: S. Fischer/S. Fischer Verlag, 1986.

Freud, Sigmund (1902b). Letter to Wilhelm Fliess, 11 March. In Sigmund Freud, *The Complete Letters of Sigmund Freud to Wilhelm Fliess: 1887–1904*, Jeffrey Moussaieff Masson (Ed.), Lottie Newman, Marianne Loring, and Jeffrey Moussaieff Masson (Transls.), pp. 455–457. Cambridge, MA: Belknap Press of Harvard University Press, 1985.

Freud, Sigmund (1904). *Zur Psychopathologie des Alltagslebens: (Über Vergessen, Versprechen, Vergreifen, Aberglaube und Irrtum)*. Berlin: Verlag von S. Karger.

Freud, Sigmund (1907). *Zur Psychopathologie des Alltagslebens: (Über Vergessen, Versprechen, Vergreifen, Aberglaube und Irrtum). Zweite, vermehrte Auflage*. Berlin: Verlag von S. Karger.

Freud, Sigmund (1909a). Untitled Contribution. [Page-Heading Titles: Die Ablösung des Kindes von den Eltern; Die Familienromane der Neurotiker; Die neurotischen Phantasien von hoher Abkunft; Deutung und Rechtfertigung dieser Phantasien; Der Familienroman wird]. In Otto Rank, *Der Mythus von der Geburt des Helden: Versuch einer psychologischen Mythendeutung*, pp. 64–68. Vienna: Franz Deuticke.

Freud, Sigmund (1909b). Family Romances, James Strachey (Transl.). In Sigmund Freud, *Collected Papers: Volume V*, James Strachey (Ed.), pp. 74–78. London: Hogarth Press and the Institute of Psycho-Analysis, 1950.

Freud, Sigmund (1909c). Family Romances, James Strachey (Transl.). In Sigmund Freud, *The Standard Edition of the Complete Psychological Works of Sigmund Freud: Volume IX. (1906–1908). Jensen's "Gradiva" and Other Works*, James Strachey, Anna Freud, Alix Strachey, and Alan Tyson (Eds. and Transls.), pp. 237–241. London: Hogarth Press and the Institute of Psycho-Analysis, 1959.

Freud, Sigmund (1910a). *Eine Kindheitserinnerung des Leonardo da Vinci*. Vienna: Franz Deuticke.

Freud, Sigmund (1910b). Letter to Carl Gustav Jung, 3 December. In Sigmund Freud and Carl Gustav Jung, *Briefwechsel*, William McGuire and Wolfgang Sauerländer (Eds.), pp. 415–418. Frankfurt am Main: S. Fischer/S. Fischer Verlag, 1974.

Freud, Sigmund (1910c). Letter to Carl Gustav Jung, 3 December. In Sigmund Freud and Carl Gustav Jung, *The Freud/Jung Letters: The Correspondence Between Sigmund Freud and C.G. Jung*, William McGuire (Ed.), Ralph Manheim and Richard F.C. Hull (Transls.), pp. 375–378. Princeton, NJ: Princeton University Press, 1974.

Freud, Sigmund (1917). Eine Kindheitserinnerung aus "Dichtung und Wahrheit". *Imago*, 5, 49–57.

Freud, Sigmund (1918a). Aus der Geschichte einer infantilen Neurose. In *Sammlung kleiner Schriften zur Neurosenlehre: Vierte Folge*, pp. 578–717. Vienna: Hugo Heller und Compagnie.

Freud, Sigmund (1918b). From the History of an Infantile Neurosis, Alix Strachey and James Strachey (Transls.). In Sigmund Freud, *The*

Standard Edition of the Complete Psychological Works of Sigmund Freud: Volume XVII. (1917–1919). An Infantile Neurosis and Other Works, James Strachey, Anna Freud, Alix Strachey, and Alan Tyson (Eds. and Transls.), pp. 7–122. London: Hogarth Press and the Institute of Psycho-Analysis, 1955.

Freud, Sigmund (1920a). Über die psychogenese eines Falles von weiblicher Homosexualität. *Internationale Zeitschrift für Psychoanalyse, 6,* 1–24.

Freud, Sigmund (1920b). The Psychogenesis of a Case of Homosexuality in a Woman, Barbara Low, R. Gabler, and James Strachey (Transls.). In Sigmund Freud, *The Standard Edition of the Complete Psychological Works of Sigmund Freud: Volume XVIII. (1920–1922). Beyond the Pleasure Principle. Group Psychology and Other Works*, James Strachey, Anna Freud, Alix Strachey, and Alan Tyson (Eds. and Transls.), pp. 147–172. London: Hogarth Press and the Institute of Psycho-Analysis, 1955.

Freud, Sigmund (1925). Personal Communication to Marie Bonaparte. n.d. Quoted in Ernest Jones, *The Life and Work of Sigmund Freud: Volume 2. Years of Maturity. 1901–1919*, p. 397. New York: Basic Books, 1955.

Freud, Sigmund (1933a). *Neue Folge der Vorlesungen zur Einführung in die Psychoanalyse.* Vienna: Internationaler Psychoanalytischer Verlag.

Freud, Sigmund (1933b). *New Introductory Lectures on Psycho-Analysis*, James Strachey (Transl.). In Sigmund Freud, *The Standard Edition of the Complete Psychological Works of Sigmund Freud: Volume XXII. (1932–36). New Introductory Lectures on Psycho-Analysis and Other Works*, James Strachey, Anna Freud, Alix Strachey, and Alan Tyson (Eds. and Transls.), pp. 5–182. London: Hogarth Press and the Institute of Psycho-Analysis, 1964.

Freud, Sigmund (1935). Letter to Theodor Reik, 4 January. In Theodor Reik, *The Haunting Melody: Psychoanalytic Experiences in Life and Music*, pp. 342–343. New York: Farrar, Straus and Young, 1953.

Freud, Sigmund (1936). Letter to Marie Bonaparte, 17 December. Box 5. Freud Museum London, Swiss Cottage, London.

Freud, Sigmund (1938). Letter to Max Eitingon, circa 7 June. In Sigmund Freud and Max Eitingon, *Briefwechsel: 1906–1939. Zweiter Band*, Michael Schröter (Ed.), pp. 901–903. Tübingen: edition diskord, 2004.

Gaither, Catherine; Kent, Jonathan; Bethard, Jonathan; Vasquez, Victor; and Rosales, Teresa (2016). Precious Gifts: Mortuary Patterns and the Shift from Animal to Human Sacrifice at Santa Rita B in the Middle Chao Valley, Peru. In Haagen D. Klaus and Marla J. Toyne (Eds.), *Ritual Violence in the Ancient Andes: Reconstructing Sacrifice on the North Coast of Peru*, pp. 150–177. Austin, TX: University of Texas Press.

Garma, Angel (1975). Discussion. *Psychoanalytic Forum*, 5, 101–103. New York: International Universities Press.

Gilliland, Robert M. (1975). Discussion. *Psychoanalytic Forum*, 5, 103–105. New York: International Universities Press.

Greenson, Ralph R. (1978). Special Problems in Psychotherapy with the Rich and Famous. Box 2. Folder 19. Ralph R. Greenson Collection. Department of Special Collections, University of California at Los Angeles, Los Angeles, California, U.S.A. Cited in Donald Spoto, *Marilyn Monroe: The Biography*. New York: HarperCollins Publishers, 1993.

Griffin, Stephen (2003). Movie Props. *Weekend F.T. Financial Times*, 1 March, p. 28.

Grinker, Roy R. (1940). Reminiscences of a Personal Contact with Freud. *American Journal of Orthopsychiatry*, 10, 850–854.

Gritten, David (2002). *Fame: Stripping Celebrity Bare*. London: Allen Lane/Penguin Books.

Grizzelle, Eva C. (1939). Letter to Sigmund Freud, 22 June. Box 23. Freud Museum London, Swiss Cottage, London.

Grun, Bernard (1971). Footnote 1. In Alban Berg, *Alban Berg: Letters to*

His Wife, Bernard Grun (Ed. and Transl.), p. 335. London: Faber & Faber.

Hall, Edward (1548). *The Vnion of the Two Noble and Illustre Famelies of Lancastre & Yorke, Beeyng Long in Continual Discension for the Croune of This Noble Realme, with all the Actes Done in Bothe the Tymes of the Princes, Bothe of the One Linage and of the Other, Beginnyng at the Tyme of Kyng Henry the Fowerth, the First Aucthor of this Deuision, and so Succesfully Proceadyng to the Reigne of the High and Prudent Prince Kyng Henry the Eight, the Vndubitate Flower and Very Heire of Both the Sayd Linages.* In *Hall's Chronicle; Containing the History of England, During the Reign of Henry the Fourth, and the Succeeding Monarchs, to the End of the Reign of Henry the Eighth, in Which are Particularly Described the Manners and Customs of Those Periods: Carefully Collated with the Editions of 1548 and 1550.* London: J. Johnson/F.C. and J. Rivington/T. Payne/Wilkie and Robson/Longman, Hurst, Rees and Orme/Cadell and Davies/J. Mawman, 1809.

Haslip, Joan (1987). *Marie Antoinette.* London: Weidenfeld & Nicolson/ George Weidenfeld & Nicolson.

Hattersley, Giles (2009). All Together Now. *The Sunday Times*, 13 December, p. 18.

Heimann, Paula (1975). Discussion. *Psychoanalytic Forum*, *5*, 109–118. New York: International Universities Press.

Helmholz, Richard H. (1975). Infanticide in the Province of Canterbury During the Fifteenth Century. *History of Childhood Quarterly*, *2*, 379–390.

Hensher, Philip (2003). Sell Sadie, Buy Zoe. *G-2. The Guardian*, 25 February, pp. 6–7.

Hoare, Philip (1990). *Serious Pleasures: The Life of Stephen Tennant.* London: Hamish Hamilton/Penguin Group.

Hocquenghem, Anne Marie (2008). Sacrifices and Ceremonial Calendars in Societies of the Central Andes: A Reconsideration. In Steve Bourget and Kimberly L. Jones (Eds.), *The Art and Archaeology of the Moche: An Ancient Andean Society of the Peruvian North Coast*, pp. 23–42. Austin, TX: University of Texas Press.

Hyde, Marina (2009). *Celebrity: How Entertainers Took Over the World and Why We Need an Exit Strategy*. London: Harvill Secker.

Inglis, Fred (2010). *A Short History of Celebrity*. Princeton, NJ: Princeton University Press.

James, Clive (1993). *Fame in the 20th Century*. London: BBC Books/ BBC Enterprises.

Jones, Ernest (1910). Letter to Sigmund Freud, 4 May. In Sigmund Freud and Ernest Jones, *The Complete Correspondence of Sigmund Freud and Ernest Jones: 1908–1939*, R. Andrew Paskauskas (Ed.), Frauke Voss (Transl.), pp. 54–57. Cambridge, MA: Belknap Press of Harvard University Press, 1993.

Jones, Ernest (1928). Letter to Sigmund Freud, 20 October. In Sigmund Freud and Ernest Jones, *The Complete Correspondence of Sigmund Freud and Ernest Jones: 1908–1939*, R. Andrew Paskauskas (Ed.), Frauke Voss (Transl.), pp. 650–651. Cambridge, MA: Belknap Press of Harvard University Press, 1993.

Jones, Ernest (1953). *The Life and Work of Sigmund Freud: Volume 1. The Formative Years and the Great Discoveries. 1856–1900*. New York: Basic Books.

Jones, Ernest (1955). *The Life and Work of Sigmund Freud: Volume 2. Years of Maturity. 1901–1919*. New York: Basic Books.

Jones, Ernest (1957). *The Life and Work of Sigmund Freud: Volume 3. The Last Phase. 1919–1939*. New York: Basic Books.

Jung, Carl Gustav (1908a). Letter to Sigmund Freud, 11 November. In Sigmund Freud and Carl Gustav Jung, *Briefwechsel*, William McGuire and Wolfgang Sauerländer (Eds.), pp. 195–197. Frankfurt am Main: S. Fischer/S. Fischer Verlag, 1974.

Jung, Carl Gustav (1908b). Letter to Sigmund Freud, 11 November. In Sigmund Freud and Carl Gustav Jung, *The Freud/Jung Letters: The Correspondence Between Sigmund Freud and C.G. Jung*, William

McGuire (Ed.), Ralph Manheim and Richard F.C. Hull (Transls.), pp. 176–177. Princeton, NJ: Princeton University Press, 1974.

Kahr, Brett (1991). The Sexual Molestation of Children: Historical Perspectives. *Journal of Psychohistory*, *19*, 191–214.

Kahr, Brett (1993). Ancient Infanticide and Modern Schizophrenia: The Clinical Uses of Psychohistorical Research. *Journal of Psychohistory*, *20*, 267–273.

Kahr, Brett (1994a). The Historical Foundations of Ritual Abuse: An Excavation of Ancient Infanticide. In Valerie Sinason (Ed.), *Treating Survivors of Satanist Abuse*, pp. 45–56. London: Routledge.

Kahr, Brett (1994b). A.P.P. Conference on Satanist Abuse: Psychodynamic Perspectives, 4 December 1993. *Bulletin of the Association of Child Psychotherapists*, *34*, 13–15.

Kahr, Brett (1994c). Child Abuse Has an Ancient History. *The Independent*, 2 May, p. 19.

Kahr, Brett (1996a). Foetal Trauma and National Disaster: A British Perspective. *Journal of Psychohistory*, *23*, 406–409.

Kahr, Brett (1996b). Book Review of Valerie Sinason (Ed.), *Treating Survivors of Satanist Abuse*. *Tavistock and Portman Gazette*, Autumn, 69–70.

Kahr, Brett (1996c). Interview with Jonathan Pedder, 22 October.

Kahr, Brett (1997). Book Review of Valerie Sinason (Ed.), *Treating Survivors of Satanist Abuse*. *Journal of Psychohistory*, *24*, 417–421.

Kahr, Brett (2001). The Legacy of Infanticide. *Journal of Psychohistory*, *29*, 40–44.

Kahr, Brett (2002a). Donald Woods Winnicott: The Cartographer of Infancy. In Brett Kahr (Ed.), *The Legacy of Winnicott: Essays on Infant and Child Mental Health*, pp. 1–10. London: Karnac Books/Other Press.

Kahr, Brett (2002b). Multiple Personality Disorder and Schizophrenia: An Interview with Professor Flora Rheta Schreiber. In Valerie Sinason (Ed.), *Attachment, Trauma and Multiplicity: Working with*

Dissociative Identity Disorder, pp. 240–264. London: Brunner-Routledge.

Kahr, Brett (2002c). Family Romance. In Edward Erwin (Ed.), *The Freud Encyclopedia: Theory, Therapy, and Culture*, pp. 187–188. New York: Routledge.

Kahr, Brett (2005). Why Freud Turned Down $25,000: Mental Health Professionals in the Witness Box. *American Imago*, *62*, 365–371.

Kahr, Brett (2006). Filming Sexual Fantasies. *American Imago*, *63*, 227–233.

Kahr, Brett (2007a). *Sex and the Psyche*. London: Allen Lane/Penguin Books, Penguin Group.

Kahr, Brett (2007b). Why Freud Turned Down $25,000. In Jane Ryan (Ed.), *Tales of Psychotherapy*, pp. 5–9. London: Karnac Books.

Kahr, Brett (2007c). The Infanticidal Attachment. *Attachment: New Directions in Psychotherapy and Relational Psychoanalysis*, *1*, 117–132.

Kahr, Brett (2007d). The Infanticidal Attachment in Schizophrenia and Dissociative Identity Disorder. *Attachment: New Directions in Psychotherapy and Relational Psychoanalysis*, *1*, 305–309.

Kahr, Brett (2008). *Who's Been Sleeping in Your Head?: The Secret World of Sexual Fantasies*. New York: Basic Books/Perseus Books Group.

Kahr, Brett (2009). Psychoanalysis and Sexpertise. In Christopher Clulow (Ed.), *Sex, Attachment, and Couple Psychotherapy: Psychoanalytic Perspectives*, pp. 1–23. London: Karnac Books.

Kahr, Brett (2012). The Infanticidal Origins of Psychosis: The Role of Trauma in Schizophrenia. In Judy Yellin and Kate White (Eds.), *Shattered States: Disorganised Attachment and Its Repair. The John Bowlby Memorial Conference Monograph 2007*, pp. 7–126. London: Karnac Books.

Kahr, Brett (2014). Television as Rorschach: The Unconscious Use of the Cathode Nipple. In Caroline Bainbridge, Ivan Ward, and Candida Yates (Eds.), *Television and Psychoanalysis: Psycho-Cultural Perspectives*, pp. 31–46. London: Karnac Books.

Kahr, Brett (2015). Erotic Tumours. Unpublished Typescript.

Kellum, Barbara A. (1974). Infanticide in England in the Later Middle Ages. *History of Childhood Quarterly*, *1*, 367–388.

Kimball, Robert (1971). Untitled Note. In Robert Kimball (Ed.), *Cole*, p. 107. New York: Holt, Rinehart and Winston.

Kimball, Robert (1983). Untitled Note to "Mister and Missus Fitch". In Cole Porter, *The Complete Lyrics of Cole Porter*, Robert Kimball (Ed.), p. 109. New York: Alfred A. Knopf.

King, Greg (1990). *Empress Alexandra: (The Last Empress of Russia)*. New York: Atlantic International Publications.

Klaus, Haagen D., and Shimada, Izumi (2016). Bodies and Blood: Middle Sicán Human Sacrifice in the Lambayeque Valley Complex (AD 900–1100). In Haagen D. Klaus and Marla J. Toyne (Eds.), *Ritual Violence in the Ancient Andes: Reconstructing Sacrifice on the North Coast of Peru*, pp. 120–149. Austin, TX: University of Texas Press.

Klein, Melanie (1957). *Envy and Gratitude: A Study of Unconscious Sources*. London: Tavistock Publications.

Lancaster, Marie-Jaqueline (Ed.) (1968). *Brian Howard: Portrait of a Failure*. London: Blond/Anthony Blond.

Langella, Frank (2012). *Dropped Names: Famous Men and Women as I Knew Them*. New York: Harper/HarperCollins Publishers.

Langer, William L. (1974). Infanticide: A Historical Survey. *History of Childhood Quarterly*, *1*, 353–365.

Langs, Robert (2002). D.W. Winnicott: The Transitional Thinker. In Brett Kahr (Ed.), *The Legacy of Winnicott: Essays on Infant and Child Mental Health*, pp. 13–22. London: Karnac Books/Other Press.

Laurents, Arthur (2012). *The Rest of the Story: A Life Completed*. Milwaukee, WI: Applause Theatre and Cinema Books/Hal Leonard Corporation.

Lidz, Theodore (1973). *The Origin and Treatment of Schizophrenic Disorders*. New York: Basic Books.

Loesser, Frank (1961). Brotherhood of Man. In *The Complete Lyrics of Frank Loesser*, Robert Kimball and Steve Nelson (Eds.), pp. 222–223. New York: Alfred A. Knopf/Random House, 2003.

Lyman, Richard B., Jr. (1974). Barbarism and Religion: Late Roman and Early Medieval Childhood. In Lloyd deMause (Ed.), *The History of Childhood*, pp. 75–100. New York: Psychohistory Press, Division of Atcom.

MacCarthy, Fiona (2002). *Byron: Life and Legend*. London: John Murray/ John Murray (Publishers).

Macfarlane, Aidan (1975). Olfaction in the Development of Social Preferences in the Human Neonate. In *Parent–Infant Interaction: Ciba Foundation Symposium 33 (New Series)*, pp. 103–113. Amsterdam: Elsevier/Excerpta Medica/North-Holland/Associated Scientific Publishers/American Elsevier.

MacRury, Iain, and Rustin, Michael (2014). *The Inner World of Doctor Who: Psychoanalytic Reflections in Time and Space*. London: Karnac Books.

Marilyn Monroe: 17, 18 & 19 November 2016. Los Angeles, CA. Auction Results (2016). Julien's Auctions [http://www.juliensauctions. com/auctions/2016/marilyn-monroe/results.html; Accessed on 12 April, 2017].

Marwick, Alice E. (2013). *Status Update: Celebrity, Publicity, and Branding in the Social Media Age*. New Haven, CT: Yale University Press.

Marx, Samuel, and Clayton, Jan (1976). *Rodgers and Hart: Bewitched, Bothered, and Bedeviled*. New York: G.P. Putnam's Sons.

Maxwell, Elsa (1954). *R.S.V.P.: Elsa Maxwell's Own Story*. Boston, MA: Little, Brown and Company.

McLaughlin, Mary Martin (1974). Survivors and Surrogates: Children and Parents from the Ninth to the Thirteenth Centuries. In Lloyd deMause (Ed.), *The History of Childhood*, pp. 101–181. New York: Psychohistory Press, Division of Atcom.

Menninger, Karl A. (1937). Letter to William C. Menninger, Charles F. Menninger, and John R. Stone, 27 February. In *The Selected Correspondence of Karl A. Menninger, 1919–1945*, Howard J. Faulkner and Virginia D. Pruitt (Eds.), pp. 235–238. New Haven, CT: Yale University Press, 1988.

Miles, Richard (2010). *Carthage Must be Destroyed: The Rise and Fall of an Ancient Mediterranean Civilization.* London: Allen Lane/Penguin Books.

Miller, Hugh (2001). *More Secrets of the Dead.* London: Channel 4 Books/Macmillan Publishers.

Miller, Milton L. (1975). Discussion. *Psychoanalytic Forum, 5,* 105–107. New York: International Universities Press.

Moore, Thomas (1833). *Letters and Journals of Lord Byron: With Notices of His Life, Vol. I.* Paris: Baudry's European Library.

Moore, Thomas (1838). *Life, Letters, and Journals of Lord Byron: Complete in One Volume. With Notes.* London: John Murray.

Mordden, Ethan (2010). *The Guest List: How Manhattan Defined American Sophistication—From the Algonquin Round Table to Truman Capote's Ball.* New York: St. Martin's Press.

Mosley, Leonard (1976). *Lindbergh: A Biography.* Garden City, NY: Doubleday and Company.

Mullen, Paul E.; James, David V.; Meloy, J. Reid; Pathé, Michele T.; Farnham, Frank R.; Preston, Lulu; Darnley, Brian; and Berman, Jeremy (2009). The Fixated and the Pursuit of Public Figures. *Journal of Forensic Psychiatry and Psychology, 20,* 33–47.

Nicolson, Harold (1931). Diary Entry, 1 October. In *Diaries and Letters: 1930–1939,* Nigel Nicolson (Ed.), p. 93. London: Collins/William Collins and Sons, 1966.

Nijinsky, Romola (1933). *Nijinsky.* London: Victor Gollancz.

Niven, David (1975). *Bring on the Empty Horses.* New York: G.P. Putnam's Sons.

Norman, Philip (2008). *John Lennon: The Life.* London: HarperCollins Publishers.

Oberlerchner, Herwig, and Tögel, Christfried (2015). Freud in Kärnten—Eine Recherche. *Luzifer-Amor, 28* (55), 158–168.

Payne, Tom (2009). *Fame: From the Bronze Age to Britney*. London: Vintage Books.

Phillips, Marie (2007). *Gods Behaving Badly*. London: Jonathan Cape.

Porter, Cole (c. 1931). Mister and Missus Fitch. In *The Complete Lyrics of Cole Porter*, Robert Kimball (Ed.), p. 109. New York: Alfred A. Knopf, 1983.

Quennell, Peter (1935). *Byron: The Years of Fame*. London: Faber & Faber.

Rank, Otto (1909). *Der Mythus von der Geburt des Helden. Versuch einer psychologischen Mythendeutung*. Vienna: Franz Deuticke.

Rank, Otto (1914). *The Myth of the Birth of the Hero: A Psychological Interpretation of Mythology*, F. Robbins and Smith Ely Jelliffe (Transls.). New York: Journal of Nervous and Mental Disease Publishing Company.

Rex, Richard (1993). *Henry VIII and the English Reformation*. Houndmills, Basingstoke, Hampshire: Macmillan Press.

Richards, Barry (1984). Schizoid States and the Market. In Barry Richards (Ed.), *Capitalism and Infancy: Essays on Psychoanalysis and Politics*, pp. 122–166. London: Free Association Books; Atlantic Highlands, NJ: Humanities Press.

Richards, Barry (2014). "Abide with Me": Mediatised Football and Collectivised Mourning. In Caroline Bainbridge and Candida Yates (Eds.), *Media and the Inner World: Psycho-cultural Approaches to Emotion, Media and Popular Culture*, pp. 19–33. Houndmills, Basingstoke, Hampshire: Palgrave Macmillan/Macmillan Publishers.

Ries, Paul (1995). Popularise and/or be Damned: Psychoanalysis and Film at the Crossroads in 1925. *International Journal of Psycho-Analysis, 76*, 759–791.

Roazen, Paul (1993). *Meeting Freud's Family*. Amherst, MA: University of Massachusetts Press.

Saul, Leon J. (1975). Discussion. *Psychoanalytic Forum, 5*, 108. New York: International Universities Press.

Scherman, David E. (Ed.) (1975). *Life Goes to the Movies*. New York: Time-Life Books.

Schur, Max (1972). *Freud: Living and Dying*. New York: International Universities Press.

Shelton, Brad (2016). Simon Cowell Net Worth—How Rich Is Simon Cowell. *Gazette Review*. [http://gazettereview.com/2016/07/simon-cowell-net-worth-rich-simon-cowell/; Accessed on 12 April 2017].

Sinason, Valerie (2001). Children Who Kill Their Teddy Bears. In Brett Kahr (Ed.), *Forensic Psychotherapy and Psychopathology: Winnicottian Perspectives*, pp. 43–49. London: H. Karnac (Books).

Stager, Lawrence E., and Wolff, Samuel R. (1984). Child Sacrifice at Carthage: Religious Rite or Population Control? Archaeological Evidence Provides Basis for a New Analysis. *Biblical Archaeology Review, 10* (1), 31–51.

Stenn, David (1988). *Clara Bow: Runnin' Wild*. New York: Doubleday/ Bantam Doubleday Dell Publishing Group.

Sterba, Richard F. (1982). *Reminiscences of a Viennese Psychoanalyst*. Detroit, MI: Wayne State University Press.

Sterne, Laurence (1760). Letter to Dr ******, 30 January. In *The Works of Laurence Sterne: In Ten Volumes Complete. Containing, I. The Life and Opinions of Tristram Shandy, Gent. II. A Sentimental Journey Through France and Italy. III. Sermons—IV. Letters. With a Life of the Author, Written by Himself. Volume the Ninth*, pp. 16–24. London: J. Rivington and Sons/J. Dodsley/G. Kearsley/J. Johnson/G.G.J. and J. Robinson/T. Cadell/J. Murray/T. Becket/R. Baldwin/A. Strahan/W. Lowndes/G. and T. Wilkie/W. Bent/D. Ogilvie, 1788.

Strachey, Lytton (1918). *Eminent Victorians: Cardinal Manning—Florence Nightingale—Dr Arnold—General Gordon*. London: Chatto & Windus.

Strong, Roy (1977). *The Cult of Elizabeth: Elizabethan Portraiture and Pageantry*. London: Thames & Hudson.

Symonds, John Addington (1886). *Sir Philip Sidney*. London: Macmillan and Company.

Taylor, David J. (2007). *Bright Young People: The Rise and Fall of a Generation: 1918–1940*. London: Chatto & Windus/Random House.

Thomas, Keith (2009). *The Ends of Life: Roads to Fulfilment in Early Modern England*. Oxford: Oxford University Press.

Tögel, Christfried (1999). "My Bad Diagnostic Error": Once More About Freud and Emmy v. N. (Fanny Moser). *International Journal of Psychoanalysis*, *80*, 1165–1173.

Uceda, Santiago (2008). The Priests of the Bicephalus Arc: Tombs and Effigies Found in Huaca de la Luna and Their Relation to Moche Rituals. In Steve Bourget and Kimberly L. Jones (Eds.), *The Art and Archaeology of the Moche: An Ancient Andean Society of the Peruvian North Coast*, pp. 153–178. Austin, TX: University of Texas Press.

Verano, John W. (2008). Communality and Diversity in Moche Human Sacrifice. In Steve Bourget and Kimberly L. Jones (Eds.), *The Art and Archaeology of the Moche: An Ancient Andean Society of the Peruvian North Coast*, pp. 195–213. Austin, TX: University of Texas Press.

Vine, Jeremy (2017). A Licence to Cull: We Need to Reduce the Number of Celebrities by 70 Per Cent. *Radio Times*, 2 September–8 September, p. 117.

Von Eckardt, Wolf; Gilman, Sander L.; and Chamberlin, J. Edward (1987). *Oscar Wilde's London: A Scrapbook of Vices and Virtues. 1880–1900*. Garden City, NY: Anchor Press/Doubleday and Company.

Wahl, Charles William (1974). Psychoanalysis of the Rich, the Famous and the Influential. *Contemporary Psychoanalysis*, *10*, 71–77.

Wahl, Charles William (1975a). Psychoanalysis of the Rich, the Famous, and the Influential. *Psychoanalytic Forum*, *5*, 92–98. New York: International Universities Press.

Wahl, Charles William (1975b). Author's Response. *Psychoanalytic Forum*, *5*, 118–121. New York: International Universities Press.

Wallace, Amy (1986). *The Prodigy*. New York: E.P. Dutton.

Waugh, Evelyn (1930). *Vile Bodies*. London: Chapman & Hall.

Welldon, Estela V. (2009). Dancing with Death. *British Journal of Psychotherapy*, *25*, 149–182.

Welldon, Estela V. (2011). *Playing with Dynamite: A Personal Approach to the Psychoanalytic Understanding of Perversions, Violence, and Criminality.* London: Karnac Books.

Winnicott, Donald W. (1935). The Manic Defence. In *Collected Papers: Through Paediatrics to Psycho-Analysis*, pp. 129–144. London: Tavistock Publications, 1958.

Winnicott, Donald W. (1949). Hate in the Counter-Transference. *International Journal of Psycho-Analysis, 30*, 69–74.

Winnicott, Donald W. (1969). The Use of an Object. *International Journal of Psycho-Analysis, 50*, 711–716.

Winnicott, Donald W. (1970). The Place of the Monarchy. In *Home Is Where We Start From: Essays by a Psychoanalyst*, Clare Winnicott, Ray Shepherd, and Madeleine Davis (Eds.), pp. 260–268. Harmondsworth, Middlesex: Penguin Books, 1986.

Woolf, Virginia (1924). Letter to Marjorie Joad, circa 20 July. In *A Change of Perspective: The Letters of Virginia Woolf. Volume III. 1923–1928*, Nigel Nicolson and Joanne Trautmann (Eds.), pp. 119–121. London: Hogarth Press, 1977.

Yates, Candida (2014a). Psychoanalysis and Television: Notes Towards a Psycho-Cultural Approach. In Caroline Bainbridge, Ivan Ward, and Candida Yates (Eds.), *Television and Psychoanalysis: Psycho-Cultural Perspectives*, pp. 1–28. London: Karnac Books.

Yates, Candida (2014b). Political Sport and the Sport of Politics: A Psycho-Cultural Study of Play, the Antics of Boris Johnson and the London 2012 Olympic Games. In Caroline Bainbridge and Candida Yates (Eds.), *Media and the Inner World: Psycho-cultural Approaches to Emotion, Media and Popular Culture*, pp. 34–50. Houndmills, Basingstoke, Hampshire: Palgrave Macmillan/Macmillan Publishers.

Yates, Candida (2015). *The Play of Political Culture, Emotion and Identity.* Houndmills, Basingstoke, Hampshire: Palgrave Macmillan/Macmillan Publishers.

INDEX

A Chorus Line (Nicholas Dante, James
    Kirkwood, Jr., Edward Kleban, and
    Marvin Hamlisch), 82
*A Funny Thing Happened on the Way
    to the Forum* (Larry Gelbart,
    Burt Shevelove, and Stephen
    Sondheim), 21
A Star is Born, see Une Étoile est née
Abandonment anxiety, 58
Academy Award, 25, 32, 37, 70
"Achilles", 42
"Adam Fenwick-Symes", 36
Adrian, 47
Aeneid (Homer), 40
Africans, 77
"Albert Square", 69
Alexander the Great, 40
Alexandra, Tsaritsa of Russia, 73
Alighieri, Dante, 77, 83
Allen, Steve, 5
Alzheimer's Disease, 82
American Idol, 11, 26, 27, 30, 63, 79
American Magazine, 45
American Neurological Association,
    9
Americans, 23, 34, 46, 47, 48, 62

Amonius, Andreas, 90 n. 13
Amsterdam, The Netherlands, 35
Annunciation Day, 41
Anti-Semitism, 9
Antidepressants, 83
Anxiety, 9, 13, 20, 56, 58, 67, 70, 76
Any Dream Will Do, 30
"Aphrodite", 36
Apis, 77
"Apollo", 36
Apollo rocketship, 15
Apollo's Oracle, 36
Arnold, Thomas, 39
As You Like It (William Shakespeare),
    41
Astaire, Fred, 32, 36
Athenians, 76–77, 79
Athens, Greece, 77, 79
Atlantic Ocean, 75
Australian Bush, Australia, 31
Austria, 2, 11
Austro-Prussian war, 2

Balzac, Honoré de, 2
Bangkok, Thailand, 35
Barrow, Clyde, 67

Barton, Elizabeth, 41
Bay Ridge, Brooklyn, New York, U.S.A., 46
B.B.C., London, *see* British Broadcasting Corporation, London
Beane, Douglas Carter, 36
Beatles, 4, 32, 33, 37
Beatty, Warren, 67
Beaufort, Margaret, Countess of Richmond and Derby, 41
Beckham, David, 52
Beckham, Victoria Adams, 52
Beijing, People's Republic of China, 35
Ben and Jerry's, 4
Bennett, Constance, 46
Berg, Alban, 5
Berkeley, George, 85
Berlin, Germany, 35
Bernays, Martha, *see* Freud, Martha Bernays
"Betty Lou", 46
Big Brother, 63
Bion, Wilfred, 55
Blair, David, 44–45
Blair, Tony, 31
Blount, William, Lord Mountjoy, 41, 90 n. 13
Bogart, Humphrey, 27
Bonaparte, Marie, 2, 6, 7, 61
Bond, Jennie, 31
Bond Street, London, 36
Bonnie and Clyde, 67
Booth, Lauren, 31
Borderline personality disorder, 20
Bourget, Steve, 78
Bow, Clara Gordon, 46
Bowie, David, 37
Boyle, Susan, 26
Braudy, Leo, 40, 52, 75
Bremen, Germany, 8
Brexit, 4
"Bright Young Things", 48

Britain's Got Talent, 85
Britain's Sexual Fantasies, 69
British Broadcasting Corporation, London, 3, 30, 31, 62, 64, 79
British Psycho-Analytical Society, London, 54
British Sexual Fantasy Research Project, 34–35
British Union of Fascists, 21
Britons, 26, 34, 62, 86
Broadway, New York, New York, U.S.A., 36
Brook Street, London, 48
Brown, Gordon, 31
Brown Derby, Los Angeles, California, U.S.A., 46.
Buckingham Palace, London, 55
Budapest, Hungary, 10
Bullitt, William, 6
Bullock, Sandra, 37
Byron, Lord, *see* Gordon, George, Lord Byron
Byromania, 44

Café de Paris, London, 18
"Café Society", 90 n. 7
California, U.S.A., 32, 35, 40, 73
Cameron, David, 31
Cameron, James, 25
Canada, 2, 32
Cara, Irene, 70
Carlsbad, Germany, *see* Karlsbad, Germany
Carthaginians, 78
"Cassie", 82
Castration anxiety, 67–68, 76
Cathode nipple, 26
Celebdaq, 64
Celebrification, 12, 34, 51
Celebrity, 5–7, 9, 11, 12, 13, 15, 17, 18, 20, 21, 22, 23, 25, 26, 27–30, 31, 32–33, 34–38, 39–40, 41, 42, 43, 44, 45, 46, 47–49, 51–53, 55,

56, 57–59, 61, 62, 63, 64, 65, 66, 67, 68, 69, 71, 72, 73, 74, 76, 79, 80, 81–82, 83, 84, 86–87, 89 n. 1, 90 n. 7

Celebrity culture, 5, 11, 12, 24, 48, 53, 54, 59, 83

Celebrity television programmes, 27–30

Celebrity worship, 12, 25–38, 39, 62–63, 65–66, 80, 83

Celebrity Worship Syndrome, 12, 25, 37, 39

Celebrity-stalking, 74

Celebrity-worship, 12, 25, 35, 37, 39, 45, 58, 62–66, 80, 83

Celts, 77

Central London, London, 48

Central News Network, 4, 24

Chaplin, Charlie, 22

Chapman, Mark David, 75

Chaucer, Geoffrey, 40, 90 n. 11

Child psychiatry, 54, 84

Child psychoanalysis, 68

Child psychology, 63

Childe Harold's Pilgrimage (George Gordon, Lord Byron), 44

Chinese, 77

"Cholly Knickerbocker", *see* Paul, Maury

Christian Science, 10

Christie's, New York, New York, U.S.A., 27

Cinema, *see* Film

Cinema Shop, 47

Clairol, 26

Clanvowe, John, 51

Clare, John, 81

Claudius, 72

Clegg, Nick, 31

Cleisthenes, 79

Climate change, 4

C.N.N., *see* Central News Network

Coca-Cola Company, 26

Cole, Cheryl, 79

Collins, Joseph, 9–10

Conciergerie, Paris, 43

Confidentiality, 21

Connell, Walter Thomas, 1, 2

Cooper, Diana, 21

Cooper, Gary, 73

Coronation Street, 48, 68, 69

Court Circular, 54–56

Covent Garden, London, 70

Coward, Noël, 17–19, 33–34, 37, 81–82

Cowell, Simon, 26

Crawford, Joan, 47

Crete, 76–77

Cruise, Tom, 34

Crystal Palace, London, 44

Curie, Marie, 84

Curtis, John Hughes, 75

Cybersex, 3

Daily Excess, 36

"Das Mädchen von Orleans" (Friedrich Schiller), 64

Daydreams, 53

de Talleyrand-Périgord, Hélie, 35

Death anxiety, 70–71

Death pool, 71

Death wishes, 58, 71, 74, 78

deMause, Lloyd, 77

Denmark, 2

Depression (clinical symptom), 20

Depression (era of American history), 47

Deprivation, 23

Der Mythus von der Geburt des Helden: Versuch einer psychologischen Mythendeutung (Otto Rank), 53

Desperate Housewives, 68

Developmental psychology, 13, 65

Diana, Princess of Wales, 34

Dickinson, Emily, 44

Diderot, Denis, 43

Die Jungfrau von Orleans (Friedrich Schiller), 64
Dietrich, Marlene, 17, 19
Dionne quintuplets, 8
Donovan, Jason, 31
"Don't Put Your Daughter on the Stage, Mrs Worthington" (Noël Coward), 81–82
Dorchester Hotel, London, 18
"Dorothy Gale", 27, 80
Double Fantasy (John Lennon and Yoko Ono), 75
Douglas-Home, Alec, 32
Downey, Robert, Jr., 71
Dracula, 19
Dreams, 8, 9, 89 n. 5
Dunaway, Faye, 67

Earthquake, 91 n. 21
EastEnders, 68, 69
Edward VIII, 7
Egyptians, 77
Einstein, Albert, 84
Eliot, Charles, 45
Elizabeth, Viscountess Castlerosse, 21
Elizabeth II, 18
Elizabethans, 41–42
Elmhirst, Susanna Isaacs, 68–69
Elsworthy Road, Primrose Hill, London, 8
Elyot, Thomas, 42–43
Eminem, 71
Encyclopaedia Britannica, 8
England, 8, 41, 45
Envy, 15, 22, 71–75, 76
Erasmus, Desiderius, 41, 90 n. 13
Etruscans, 77
Europa, 76
Exhibitionism, 12, 21, 22, 23, 34, 39

Facebook, 3
Fairbanks, Douglas, 45
Falconet, Étienne Maurice, 43

Fame, 5–8, 10, 11, 12, 13, 15, 17, 19, 20, 22, 25, 26, 29–30, 37, 39–46, 48–49, 51–53, 61, 62, 63, 64, 66, 67, 68, 69, 70, 72, 76, 81–82, 83, 84–85, 86, 87, 89 n. 3, 89 n. 4, 90 n. 7, 90 n. 9
"Fame" (allegorical figure), 42
Fame (film), 70
"Fame" (song), 70
Fame Academy, 29, 30
"Fame and Fortune Contest", 46
Fame-worship, 13, 45, 48, 58, 66
Family romance, 13, 54, 62, 66, 67, 70–71, 76, 90 n. 17, 90 n. 18, 91 n. 20
"Family Romances" (Sigmund Freud), 53
Fans, 13, 33, 45, 55, 57, 58, 63, 73, 74, 75, 82, 83, 90 n. 7
Fantasy, 66
Fawcett, Farrah, 66
Ferenczi, Sándor, 10
Fetishism, 34
Film, 10–11, 13, 15, 16, 19, 22, 25, 27, 32, 34, 36, 45, 46, 47, 48, 52, 53, 57, 59, 65, 66, 67, 69, 70, 73, 74, 79, 81, 82, 83, 85, 91 n. 21
Financial Times, 26
Fliess, Wilhelm, 7
Ford, Harrison, 26–27
Ford Motor Company, 26
Forensic psychiatry, 64
Forensic psychoanalysis, 64
Forensic psychotherapy, 64
42nd Street, 47
France, 43, 72, 78
Franz Josef, 8, 89 n. 5
"Frau X", 53
Frazier, Brenda Diana Duff, 90 n. 7
Freud, Anna, 2
Freud, Harry, 3
Freud, Martha Bernays, 7
Freud, Sigmund, 1–13, 16, 53–54, 59, 61–65, 70, 87, 89 n. 6, 91 n. 21

Freudianism, 51

Freudism, 9

Gable, Clark, 57–58

Gaius Plinius Secundus, *see* Pliny the
    Elder

Garbo, Greta, 73

Garland, Judy, 27, 32

Garnett, Bunny, 17

George VI, 3

George Washington, 8

Geheimnisse einer Seele, 10

Germans, 3

Germany, 2

Gere, Richard, 74

Gilbert, William Schwenck, 44

Global warming, 4

Globe Theatre, London, 69

Gods Behaving Badly (Marie Phillips),
    36

Goldwyn, Samuel, 11

Google, 4

Gordon, George, Lord Byron, 44, 47

Gore, Michael, 70

Gospel Oak Schools, London, 84

Grable, Betty, 66

Grandiosity, 16, 21, 39

Grant, Hugh, 64

Great Britain, 3, 26, 48

Great War, 2

Greece, 2

Greeks, 77

Grinker, Roy, Sr., 11

Grizzelle, Eva, 1–2

Group sex, 34

Guillotine, 78

Habsburgs, 52

Hagen, Jean, 83

Hale, Sonnie, 48

Hamburg, Germany, 9

Hanks, Tom, 34

"Happy Birthday" (Patty Hill and
    Mildred Hill), 27

Harry Potter and the Goblet of Fire, 19

Harvard University, Cambridge,
    Massachusetts, U.S.A., 9, 45

Hatred, 9, 22, 58

Hearst, William Randolph, 11

Heat, 66

Hébert, Jacques-René, 72

Hebrews, 77

Hecht, Ben, 46

Hello!, 54, 55

Henry VII, 40–41

Henry VIII, 41

Hepburn, Katharine, 71

Herakles, 79

Herodotus, 40

"Herr X", 53

Hesiod, 40

Hill, Denis, 3

Hilton, Paris, 66

Hindus, 77

Hiroshima, Japan, 4

Histrionic personality disorder, 82

Hitler, Adolf, 4

H.M.S. Courageous, 3

Hoboken, New Jersey, U.S.A., 8

Hohenzollerns, 52

Hollywood, California, U.S.A., 11, 16,
    32, 35, 37, 46, 57, 59, 65, 67, 73,
    91 n. 21

Hollywood Hotel, 46

Holy Maid of Ipswich, 41

Holy Maid of Kent, *see* Barton,
    Elizabeth

Holy Maid of Leominster, 41

Homer, 40

Hong Kong, Hong Kong Special
    Administrative Region of the
    People's Republic of China, 35

"Hooray for Hollywood" (Johnny
    Mercer and Dick Whiting), 46

Hope, Bob, 71

Horse Feathers, 57

"Hous of Fame" (Geoffrey Chaucer),
    40, 90 n. 11

"House of Fame" (Geoffrey Chaucer), *see* "Hous of Fame" (Geoffrey Chaucer)
How Do You Solve a Problem Like Maria?, 30
Hungary, 35
Hunger Games, 79
Hurley, Elizabeth, 39
Hydrotherapy, 10
Hysteria, 7, 89 n. 5

"I Am" (John Clare), 81
Ich bin ein Star—Holt mich hier raus!, 31
Iliad (Homer), 40
I'll Do Anything, 30
I'm a Celebrity . . . Get Me Out of Here!, 27, 30–31, 63
Immigration crisis, 4
"Impersonation Party", 48
Impotence, 13, 67–68, 76
In Bloom, 66
"Indiana Jones", 27
Infanticide, 13, 76–80, 91 n. 21
Inferno, La Divina Commedia (Dante Alighieri), 77
Instagram, 4
Intellectual disability, 68
Internal objects, 55
Interpretation, 57
Intrapsychic conflict, 39
Ioseph, Mighell, 40–41
Istanbul, Turkey, 35
It, 46
"It's Only a Paper Moon" (Harold Arlen, Edgar Yipsel ("Yip") Harburg, and Billy Rose), 46
iTunes, 4, 66

Jackson, Glenda, 32
James, Clive, 52
Japanese, 77
"Jaques", 42
Je suis une célébrité—sortez-moi de là!, 31
Jeopardy, 82

Jewry, 11
John, Elton, 34
Jones, Ernest, 8, 9
"Julian Marsh", 47
Jung, Carl Gustav, 1, 10

Kansas, U.S.A., 59
Karlsbad, Germany, 35
Kay, Peter, 30
Keeler, Ruby, 47
Kellogg, 26
Kelly, Gene, 32
Kennedy, John Fitzgerald, 27
Kimball, Robert, 90 n. 10
Kindle, 4
Klein, Melanie, 72
Knossos, Crete, 77
Knowles, Beyoncé, 66
Konigsvilla, Karlsbad, Germany, 35

La Divina Commedia (Dante Alighieri), 77, 83
La Ferme: Célébrités en Afrique, 31
La Peau de chagrin: Roman philosophique (Honoré de Balzac), 2
Lady Gaga, 21
"Lady Macbeth", 18
Lady Olivier, *see* Leigh, Vivien
Lane, Nathan, 21
Langella, Frank, 19, 81
Langs, Robert, 56–57
Las Vegas, Nevada, U.S.A., 35
Laurents, Arthur, 22
Law, Jude, 32
Laye, Evelyn, 48
Le Roy, Illinois, U.S.A., 1
Leigh, Vivien, 18–19
Lennon, John, 32, 52, 75
Leonardo da Vinci, 6, 64
Leopold, Nathan, Jr., 11
Let's Be Famous, 48
Letty Lynton, 47
"Lina Lamont", 83
Lindbergh, Charles Augustus, 74–75

Lindbergh, Charles Augustus, Jr., 74–75
" 'Living Celebrity' party", 48
Lloyd, Harold, 46
Lloyd Webber, Andrew, Baron Lloyd Webber of Sydmonton, 30, 80
Loeb, Richard, 11
Loewenstein, Rudolph, 67
London, 1, 3, 8, 11, 15, 34, 45, 48, 73
Loneliness, 10, 18, 45, 68–70, 76
Lord Byron, see Gordon, George, Lord Byron
Los Angeles, California, U.S.A., 22
Louis Charles, 72
Lucius Mestrius Plutarchus, see Plutarch
"Lucky Lindy", see Lindbergh, Charles Augustus
Luttrellstown Castle, Clonsilla, Dublin, Ireland, 52
"Lycidas" (John Milton), 25

Macbeth (William Shakespeare), 18
"Macbeth", 18
MacCarthy, Brendan, 84
Macfarlane, Aidan, 65
Madame Tussauds, 35
Madison Square Garden, New York, New York, U.S.A., 27
Madonna, 21
Madras, India, 2
"Maestro X", 15–16, 17
Magyars, 77
Mahler, Gustav, 5
Majestic Theatre, New York, New York, U.S.A., 21
Major Bowes Amateur Hour, 47
Make Me a Star, 46
Maltby, John, 37
Mandela, Nelson, 84
Manhattan, New York, U.S.A., see New York, New York, U.S.A
Manners, Henry, Duke of Rutland, 21–22

Maresfield Gardens, Swiss Cottage, London, 1
Marie Antoinette, 72
Marie of Roumania, 48
Martin, Steve, 37
"Mary Evans", 46
Marx Brothers, 57
Masochism, 72
Masturbation, 25, 33
Matthews, Jessie, 48
Maudsley Hospital, London, 3
Maxwell, Elsa, 73
M.B.E., see Member of the Most Excellent Order of the British Empire
McCartney, Paul, 33
McDonald's, 4
McEachran, Neil, 48
McKechnie, Donna, 82
Media psychology, 61
Mellon, Rachel "Bunny", 81
Member of the Most Excellent Order of the British Empire, 33
Menninger, Karl, 59, 65
Mental health, 20, 86
Mental health broadcasting, 62
Mental health professionals, 21, 25
Mental illness, 4
Merton of the Movies, 46
Mesoamericans, 77
Messalina, 72
Metapsychology, 58
Michael Joseph an Gof, see Mighell Ioseph
Micro-celebrity, 27
Middle Ages, 40, 77
Middle East, 16
Millennium Bridge, London, 69–70
Milton, John, 25
Minogue, Dannii, 79
Minos, 76–77
Minotaur, 77–79
Miracle Pictures, 46

Misattunement, 68–70
"Miss Y", 17
Monkey Business, 57
Monroe, Marilyn, 27
Moore, Thomas, 44
Mordden, Ethan, 90 n. 10
Moser, Fanny, 6
Mosley, Oswald, 21
Mother Teresa, 26
Motion Picture, 46
Motion Picture Classic, 46
Movie Crazy, 46
Movies, *see* Film
"Mr Chatterbox", 36
Mr. and Mrs. Fitch (Douglas Carter Beane), 36
"Mr. S. Beach Fitch", *see* "Mr. S. Beech Fitch"
"Mr. S. Beech Fitch", 35, 90 n. 10
"Mrs. S. Beach Fitch", *see* "Mrs. S. Beech Fitch"
"Mrs. S. Beech Fitch", 35, 90 n. 10
Murder, 11, 72, 74–75, 79, 80, 82
Murphy, George, 32
Mussolini, Benito, 45

Nagasaki, Japan, 4
Narcissism, 12, 16, 17, 22
Narcissistic personality disorder, 17, 20
Nashville, Tennessee, U.S.A., 35, 90 n. 7
National Portrait Gallery, London, 42
National Registration Act, United Kingdom, 3
Naturalis Historiae (Pliny the Elder), 72
Navratilova, Martina, 31
Nazis, 2, 4, 8, 11
Netanyahu, Benjamin, 16
Neuroses, 10, 20
New Delhi, India, 35

New York, New York, U.S.A., 3, 21, 22, 35, 45, 56, 70, 90 n. 7
New York City, New York, U.S.A., *see* New York, New York, U.S.A
New York Psychoanalytic Society, New York, New York, U.S.A., 56
New York Stock Exchange, New York, New York, U.S.A., 24
Nicolson, Harold, 21–22
Nielsen Company, 23
Nijinsky, Vaslav, 5
9/11, 4
Niven, David, 57–58
Nobel Prize, 35
North London, London, 36, 84
Northern Peru, Peru, 78
Notley Abbey, Haddenham, Buckinghamshire, 18
Notoriety, 9, 11, 21, 26, 39, 40, 41, 48
Notting Hill, London, 15, 73

Object loss, 63, 69, 76
Object usage, *see* Use of an object
Olivier, Laurence, 18–19
Ono, Yoko, 52
Ontario, Canada, 8
Ostrakon, 79
Over the Rainbow, 30, 79

Pabst, Georg Wilhelm, 10
Paddington Green Children's Hospital, London, 68
Pailleux, 44
Parker, Bonnie, 67
Parliament, 3, 21, 32, 89 n. 5
Pathological narcissism, 12
Pattinson, Robert, 19
Paul, Maury, 35
Pavarotti, Luciano, 34
"Peggy Sawyer", 47
Penn, Arthur, 67
Peru, 78

*Peter Kay's Britain's Got the Pop Factor
 . . . and Possibly a New Celebrity
 Jesus Christ Soapstar Superstar
 Strictly on Ice*, 30
Petros, Prince of Greece and Denmark,
 2
Phillips, Marie, 36
Pickford, Mary, 45
Pitchford, Dean, 70
Pius IX, 35
Pliny the Elder [Gaius Plinius
 Secundus], 72
Plutarch [Lucius Mestrius Plutarchus],
 40, 80
Poland, 2
Pollok, Robert, 15
Pop Idol, 27, 46, 87
Pornography, 9, 10, 90 n. 8
Porter, Cole, 35, 90 n. 10
Porter, Linda, 35
Potocka, Emanuela, 35
Power, Tyrone, 82
Prague, Czech Republic, 35
Pre-Colombians, 78
Primal scene, *see* "Urszene"
Prostitution, 64, 72
"Provna", 36
"Pseudolus", 21
Psychiatry, 3, 59, 65
Psychoanalysis, 2, 4, 5, 6, 7, 8, 9, 10, 11,
 12, 13, 16, 20, 53, 54, 55, 56–57,
 58, 59, 60, 61, 65, 67, 68, 72, 73, 78,
 83, 84, 86, 89 n. 5, 90 n. 8
Psychodynamics, 13, 39, 53
Psychogenesis, 6
Psychohistory, 77
Psychology, 5, 9, 12, 13, 20, 21, 23, 37,
 38, 53, 54, 57, 62, 67, 71, 78, 81
Psychopathology, 12, 17, 23, 89 n. 6
Psychosexuality, 21
Psychotherapy, 20, 21, 32, 62, 72, 73,
 86
Publius Vergilius Maro, *see* Virgil

Purgatorio, La Divina Commedia
 (Dante Alighieri), 83
Putnam, James Jackson, 9

Queen Mother, 55
Quintanilla-Pérez, Selena, *see* Selena
Quintus Septimius Florens
 Tertullianus, *see* Tertullian

Radio Times, 27, 37
Rank, Otto, 53
Rantzen, Esther, 31
Rapprochement subphase, 21
Rasputin, Grigori Efimovich, 73
Reagan, Ronald, 32
Reality television, 27, 39, 51, 63, 79,
 86
Règne de la Terreur, 43
Reichert-Habbishaw, Ursula, 74
Renaissance, 77
Reputation, 41–42
Romanovs, 52
Romans, 77
Rome, Italy, 35, 78
Rome Film Festival, Rome, Italy, 36
"Ronnie Bowers", 46
Royal Family, United Kingdom, 54–
 55

Sadism, 64, 74
Sadomasochism, 34
Saldívar, Yolanda, 74
Salem, Massachusetts, U.S.A., 78
Scherzinger, Nicole, 79
Schiller, Friedrich, 64
Schindler's List, 16
Schur, Max, 11
Schwarzenegger, Arnold, 32
Scott, Peggy, 45
*Secrets of a Soul, see Geheimnisse einer
 Seele*
Selena [Selena Quintanilla-Pérez], 74
Separation-individuation, 21

Sexual fantasies, 34–35, 36, 57, 62, 69–70
Sexuality, 8, 9, 19
Shadowland, 46
Shakespeare, William, 41–42
Shanghai, People's Republic of China, 35
Shedu, 77
Sibling rivalry, 62–63, 91 n. 21
Sidney, Philip, 42
Simpson, Wallis, 7
Singin' in the Rain, 83
So You Want to Be a Celebrity? (Steve Allen), 5
South London, London, 3, 69
Southern California, U.S.A., 73
Spears, Britney, 66
Spice Girls, 52
Spielberg, Steven, 16, 34
Starbucks, 3
Sterne, Laurence, 43
Sting, 21
Strachey, Lytton, 39, 86
Stratford-upon-Avon, Warwickshire, 18
Stuart, Gloria, 25
Suicide, 82
Sullivan, Arthur, 44
Sunset Boulevard, Hollywood, California, U.S.A., 59
Supernaturalism, 10
Superstar, 30
Sydney, Australia, 35
Symonds, John Addington, 42
Syria, 4
Szechenyi, Laszlo, 35

Taliban, 32
Tauber, Richard, 5
Television, 3, 11, 20, 23, 24, 26, 27–30, 31, 34, 36, 39, 47, 48, 51, 52, 62, 63, 68, 69–70, 75, 79, 84, 85, 86
Temple, Shirley, 32, 47
Tennant, Stephen, 48

Teresa, Mother, *see* Mother Teresa
Tertullian [Quintus Septimius Florens Tertullianus], 80
Texas, 74
Thatcher, Carol, 31
Thatcher, Margaret, 31
The Archers, 68
The Celebrity Circus (Elsa Maxwell), 25
The Course of Time: A Poem, in Ten Books (Robert Pollok), 15
The Dakota, New York, New York, U.S.A., 75
The Famous Hiſtorie of Troylus and Creſſeid (William Shakespeare), *see Troilus and Cressida* (William Shakespeare)
The Farm: Celebrities in Africa, *see La Ferme: Célébrités en Afrique*
The Gay Divorce (Samuel Hoffenstein, Cole Porter, Dwight Taylor, and Kenneth Webb), 35–36
The Life and Opinions of Tristram Shandy, Gentleman (Laurence Sterne), 43
The Maiden from Orleans (Friedrich Schiller), *see Die Jungfrau von Orleans* (Friedrich Schiller)
The Maltese Falcon, 27
"The Manic Defence" (Donald W. Winnicott), 54–56
The Myth of the Birth of the Hero: A Psychological Interpretation of Mythology (Otto Rank), *see Der Mythus von der Geburt des Helden: Versuch einer psychologischen Mythendeutung* (Otto Rank), 53
The New York Times, 10
The Original Amateur Hour, 47
The Poseidon Adventure, 91 n. 21
"The Psychogenesis of a Case of Homosexuality in a Woman" (Sigmund Freud), *see* "Über die

psychogenese eines Falles von weiblicher Homosexualität" (Sigmund Freud)

The Psychopathology of Everyday Life: Forgetting, Slips of the Tongue, Bungled Actions, Superstitions and Errors (Sigmund Freud), *see Zur Psychopathologie des Alltagslebens: (Über Vergessen, Versprechen, Vergreifen, Aberglaube und Irrtum)* (Sigmund Freud)

"The Rovers", 69

The Sunday Times Rich List 2010, 26

The Telegraph Magazine, 19

The Tempest (Arthur Sullivan), 44

The Times, 54

The Towering Inferno, 91 n. 21

"The Use of an Object" (Donald W. Winnicott), 56–57

The Voice, 11

The Voice UK, 28

The Wizard of Oz, 27, 80

The X Factor, 11, 27, 79, 87

Theatre, 15, 17, 21, 22, 30, 36, 41, 42, 46, 64, 69, 81, 82, 86, 90 n. 10, 91, n. 21.

Theseus, 77

Times Square, New York, New York, U.S.A., 3

Titanic, 25

Todd, Thelma, 57–58

Tony Award, 21, 82

Topeka, Kansas, U.S.A., 59

Tophet, 78

Transcendentalism, 10

Troilus and Cressida (William Shakespeare), 42

Trudeau, Pierre, 32

Trump, Donald, 4

Tudors, 41

Tufnell, Phil, 31

Tulsa, Oklahoma, U.S.A., 35

Twilight, 19

Twitter, 3

"Über die psychogenese eines Falles von weiblicher Homosexualität" (Sigmund Freud), 6

Unconscious, 12, 13, 23, 38, 53, 57, 65, 76

Une Étoile est née, 31

United Kingdom, 3, 31

United States of America, 8, 71

Universität zu Wien, Vienna, Austria, 7

University of Leicester, Leicester, Leicestershire, 37

University of Oxford, Oxford, Oxfordshire, 44–45

University of Southern California, Los Angeles, California, U.S.A., 40

University of Texas, Austin, Texas, U.S.A., 78

University of Vienna, Vienna, Austria, *see* Universität zu Wien, Vienna, Austria

Unton, Henry, 42

Upper West Side, New York, New York, U.S.A., 75

"Urszene", 59, 65

Use of an object, 13, 22, 23, 38, 52, 53, 57, 63, 65, 76

Ushi-oni, 77

Valentino, Rudolph, 45

Vendôme, Hollywood, California, U.S.A., 59, 65

Victorians, 84

Vienna, Austria, 2, 35

Vile Bodies (Evelyn Waugh), 36

Vine, Jeremy, 37

Violence, 20, 34

Virgil [Publius Vergilius Maro], 40

Virginia, U.S.A., 75

von Goethe, Johann Wolfgang, 6

Walters, Barbara, 75

Warburg, Aby, 6

Warner Brothers, 27

Warsaw, Poland, 3
Washington, D.C., U.S.A., 35
Waugh, Evelyn, 36, 48
Welldon, Estela, 64–65
Wells, Herbert George, 22
Weltkrieg, *see* Great War
West End, London, 30, 79
West London, London, 68
West Side Story (Leonard Bernstein,
    Arthur Laurents, and Stephen
    Sondheim), 22
Westminster Abbey, London, 34
Weygandt, Wilhelm, 9
What Price Hollywood?, 46
What's App, 4
Wilde, Oscar, 44–45
Wilhelm II, 6–7, 89 n. 2
William Ellis School, Highgate,
    London, 84
Williams, Robbie, 73–74
Wilson, Woodrow, 45
Winchell, Walter, 35

Winnicott, Donald W., 13, 54–57, 58,
    59, 63–64, 65, 68, 71
Witherspoon, Reese, 66
Wittelsbachs, 52
Woods, Tiger, 23–24, 37
Woolf, Virginia, 17

Xenophon, 40

YouTube, 3

"Z", 32–33
Zeta-Jones, Catherine, 36
Zur Psychopathologie des Alltagslebens:
    (Über Vergessen, Versprechen,
    Vergreifen, Aberglaube und Irrtum)
    (Sigmund Freud), 8, 89 n. 6
Zur Psychopathologie des Alltagslebens:
    (Über Vergessen, Versprechen,
    Vergreifen, Aberglaube und
    Irrtum). Zweite, vermehrte Auflage
    (Sigmund Freud), 89 n. 6

Printed in the United States
by Baker & Taylor Publisher Services